TO

My husband John
who first came to 1418 Carlisle Avenue in 1965
and who keeps the memories alive with me

And

Our daughter Lisa
who encouraged and challenged me
after reading a few of the early stories
when she said, "Well, Mom,
when are you going to put these into a book?"

Here it is for you, Lisa!

~ Contents ~

~ PREFACE ~

~ The Miracle of Memories ~

DEAR Reader,

On a beautiful summer day in 1995, I turned the gold handle of our front door for the last time. Slowly, I turned the key in the lock, hearing the gentle click for the last time. And then I walked off the front porch of 1418 Carlisle Avenue, the home I had grown up in and the only home my parents had ever owned, the home they had loved for forty-five years.

When my father had died that summer, two years after my mother, it had taken a month to empty the house. We had given away keepsakes to dear friends and family, offered unwanted items to used furniture stores like the ones my mother had frequented in her ingenious decorating days, and packed precious items to take to our own home. The days had not seemed overly sad as both of my parents had lived long lives and we had parted with each other on loving terms.

But, suddenly in those final moments after I turned the key for the last time and I walked off the porch for the last time, an avalanche of tears engulfed me. How sorrowful it was to leave! After all, the white Dutch colonial had held us three in its arms for those many years, becoming like one of us itself, until our lives were intertwined with it.

And now it was over. With my last steps, I was leaving it all behind. My heart was suddenly breaking with the thought that I had lost everything: the comforting house, my beloved parents, my own youth spent here, as well as the wonderful people whom we had lived among on that stately Avenue.

Knowing full well that the years had slowly but surely exacted their inevitable toll, with the charm of the neighborhood changing, most of the former neighbors no longer there, my parents experiencing the excruciating decline of their last years—I still wanted it all back, to return to the brightest and happiest years we had spent together here. If only we could have one more magical week together, perhaps one magical hour.

· · ·

When I reached our car at the curb, my husband was overcome with sadness as well. Why, he had known my parents and visited 1418 Carlisle Avenue himself for thirty years. But it was time to drive away, down the two blocks along Carlisle Avenue to State Street, and then home to West Bend where we lived with our daughter Lisa.

It was in those moments that I received a miracle. Without warning, my vision changed. Even as we inched away from the curb, I seemed to see my father parking his car right in front of us, briefcase in hand, with a wave and a smile for us. Joe Arnone, our next door neighbor for many years, was trimming his grass so that not one blade was out of place. As we entered the next block, there was kind Mrs. Anderson on her front porch, ready to welcome me in for my Saturday afternoon piano lesson. When we were passing Lincoln School, there was Mr. Temme, our beloved principal, getting in to his big silver-gray Buick at the end of another day. And then, oh, there was Mother, walking hand-in-hand with a little girl to Lincoln's neighborhood story hour!

I had not lost my parents... I had not lost that precious place and the precious people I had loved!

And so ever since that day many years ago now when I left 1418 Carlisle Avenue, I welcome the memories. I embrace them! I view them as a miracle as they flood my heart and mind. When I remember those days, we are still together.

. . .

But to write about them? I had not considered that until a few years ago, on one quiet summer night when "out of the clear blue" I thought: I must write the story of Philip and Jeanette, our dear friends who lived next door to us at 1422 Carlisle Avenue for too short a time.

And that is how these stories began. One after another they came to be, recollecting the life I was privileged to have because of my parents at 1418 Carlisle Avenue. They were not difficult to write because my heart was simply leading me home. As I wrote them, that precious place and those precious people and times came alive for me.

. . .

Over time, when I came to learn that my stories often helped other grown children recollect their fond memories, I considered that another miracle!

And so, dear reader, my best wishes to you, as you take my sentimental journey of memories down Carlisle Avenue and as you take your own miraculous drive down the avenue of your past!

I would love to hear from you. Please write to me at gianforteproductions@gmail.com.

Section 1

~ AT HOME ~

Our house has a heart, and a soul, and eyes to see us with; and approvals and solicitudes, and deep sympathies. It is of us, and we are in its confidence, and we live in its grace and in the peace of its benediction... We cannot enter it unmoved.

~Mark Twain

1.

~ Mother's American Home ~

WHEN a family owns the very same home for forty-five years, as mine did, that home becomes almost a living, breathing member of the family. From its purchase in 1950 until I parted with it in 1995, my parents and I came to know every nook and cranny of the old house that stood at 1418 Carlisle Avenue. We accepted and understood its every idiosyncrasy and as it aged, we took the greatest care to preserve it. Because we loved it.

In return, our house steadfastly encircled us. It shared in our joyful scenes of celebration and gave to us its sturdy arms of comfort in times of sadness. We came to feel as if it knew us and in turn, we felt as if we three were its honored guests.

. . .

Over those forty-five years, the white Dutch colonial occupied the center of hundreds, perhaps even thousands, of our conversations. It was a frequent dinner topic as I grew up and later over the many years I was to visit, as we carefully considered and planned its many repairs. When friends and relatives came to visit, the interesting old house often seemed to arise as a topic. And when we mentioned our home's address, it was frequently met with admiring comments about the lovely homes along Carlisle Avenue.

As the years unfolded, our little family often marked time by tracing its history, noting what year a certain improvement had been made or when a family event had occurred within its walls. In truth, it seemed as if we were reciting a person's biography.

Its story had begun at the turn of the century with the proud couple who built it and whose son's carved initials still remained partially visible on a wooden post in the old garage, like archeological proof of its origins. But time had inevitably moved on by the summer of 1950 and the original owner had become a widow, deciding to retire to Florida and to reluctantly leave the white colonial behind.

A second chapter in the history of 1418 Carlisle Avenue was to begin. Our family was to have the honor of taking up residence within its walls.

A second chapter in the history of 1418 Carlisle Avenue was to begin.

. . .

To buy 1418 Carlisle, however, was a frightening prospect! My parents had married "late in life" after the War and had come to Racine due to a government assignment for my father, but with the additional hope of starting his accounting business. To purchase a home at their ages and to go into debt for it, just as they started a business and a family, loomed as a tremendous risk. But 1418 was large enough to house my father's office, as doctors and dentists still placed shingles outside of their homes in those days, and large enough for an apartment to be created in the upstairs for rent. So with a borrowed down payment from my father's brother and a land contract from the original owner, my parents came to own the only home they would ever have.

. . .

With its ownership, the challenge of furnishing it began for Mother. There were not one, but two adjoining living rooms. There was an imposing front entrance hall with heavy pocket doors. Thirty windows needed her window treatments. Our home's beauty mattered greatly to her, as it would to many mothers, but in her case there was one special reason. Mother was an artist. She appreciated beauty and she needed to create it.

Mother's aqua kitchen cupboards with the gateleg table nearby

But where was the money coming from to purchase so many fine furnishings? Since that source seemed quite uncertain in those early years, Mother needed to rely on ingenious ideas! It was to the *American Home* magazine that she turned for inspiration. Large glossy issues would be filled with bookmarks of her favorite rooms. Mother would pore over them, analyzing colors and room arrangements and dreaming of what she wanted to create.

And slowly but surely Mother did collect the contents of our home. On a regular basis, she would explore the fine furnishings of Earl the Trader on State Street. Why, who knew what second-hand treasures might be found today that were not there yesterday? Perhaps a dresser sitting out on the street might catch her eye, or a lamp, no matter if the pretty shade was a bit faded! Over time Mother put together a very pleasing collection accentuated by her own beautiful paintings, which hang in my home today as priceless keepsakes.

.   .   .

However, there was one source of furnishings that preyed on Mother's mind. Although the previous owner had left 1418 Carlisle for Florida, much of her furniture had stayed behind. At the last minute, she had asked my parents to store various pieces in the basement, which she claimed would be retrieved in the very near future. Now the sheets that had been draped over that owner's collection were turned back here and there for Mother to catch just a glimpse of the contents. Why, there was a pretty pink-and-white striped comfy wing chair! Oh, there was a darling gateleg table with six matching chairs! Perhaps she should bring them upstairs to try for a few days, just to get ideas! Honest and proper, Mother struggled with her conscience.

And that is how, one by one, the stored furniture collection moved from the basement to the first and second floors of 1418. And that is how years went by of sitting in the pink wing chair and looking at the pretty gateleg table. All were just being borrowed, for the moment. Mother was ingeniously achieving her dream of The American Home.

. . .

Then one day the door bell unexpectedly rang. There stood a woman who introduced herself as the daughter of 1418 Carlisle's original owner. Mother, of course, graciously welcomed her in, even as her own heart stood still. It took just a minute or two for the visitor to cry out with indignation, "Why, that is my mother's table!"

Soon the daughter had identified this and that piece of furniture that she knew should have been stored for her mother in the basement. Leaving in a huff, despite Mother's profuse apologies, she announced that very soon indeed the furniture would be called for.

Mother's depths of mortification knew no bounds. Why, she was raised in a Lutheran church with her goal to be the perfect Christian. Each and every piece of furniture was to be moved right back to the basement! But the pink wing chair seemed so much heavier than when she had brought it up and the gateleg table set was so perfect that perhaps it could stay in its place just a day or two more.

And that is how more than forty more years went by with the borrowed furniture gracing our home, unclaimed year after year. Oh, eventually Mother was able to add a few fine new pieces. Eventually my father found a French provincial baby grand piano to rest perfectly in the front living room's bay window. A new grandfather clock chimed in the front hallway. But it was our borrowed furniture that provided much of Mother's décor.

Indeed, over those forty-five years that the white Dutch colonial was ours, the carefully chosen furnishings seemed to blend with the old house itself and in fact, to become one with us. In truth, everything about 1418 Carlisle Avenue seemed meant to be.

.   .   .

When I had the bittersweet task of saying good-bye to our 1418 Carlisle Avenue colonial, I wanted to share its charming old dressers, chairs, and tables with relatives and friends, and to return some to stores just like Earl the Trader for another owner to enjoy. (We could not trace the visiting daughter from years before!)

And it was also time to move some of the pieces and paintings to my own home. I treasure each and every one today as if they were museum quality. I know that each was selected and arranged with love by my mother, our artist in residence. I can still see every room as she left it, just as beautiful as any magazine photo.

But what I have come to see over the many years that have passed without her, is that those furnishings, beautifully arranged as they became, were insignificant in and of themselves. Instead, they are the treasured reminders of the lovely person who collected them and of the precious life we three shared with the white Dutch colonial at 1418 Carlisle Avenue.

2.

Waiting for the Fireflies

I REMEMBER warm summer nights, velvety air, huge green leaves above from the giant old maple trees, and manicured hedges. I remember the soft glow of the milk-glass street lights that stretched down our boulevard like a pearl necklace.

I remember a white frame Dutch colonial house with a big, shiny, gray floor front porch. I remember a "sunroom" in the back, with its green-and-white striped awnings. I remember the perfectly matching showy white snowball blossoms of the green hydrangea leaves at the foundation below.

I remember a collage of ferns, hollyhocks, bridal wreathe, and orange blossoms, and gardens of tall purple and white phlox. I remember borders of peony bushes in three shades (deep rose, pink and white), holding the blossoms close to my nose, drinking in the smell. *(Careful of the ants hiding within!)* I remember the ancient lilac bushes next to the back picket fence and the climbing pink rose hugging the old garage wall.

I remember voices of children floating through the air as they played across the big yards. I remember the echoing of mothers' voices calling them home when an evening grew dark.

But most of all, I remember Mother. How fortunate, fortunate beyond belief, that *she* was *my* mother. Decades later, I remember her oh, so vividly and I am thankful that she was mine, and that I was hers.

. . .

As we children dispersed after our evening games of Hide-and-Go-Seek and Tag, I would wind my way home across the yards, knowing that I would find her working in her gorgeous gardens. There was always one more bed to weed or one more bouquet for her to pick, but I knew that she always had time for me.

I remember coming home to stand near her, to visit about the day as she carefully watered a bed or two before finally giving in to the fading light. And just then, as the night gently surrounded us, I remember waiting with her for the fireflies. *Did we imagine one flickering glint?* Then, yes, another glimmer! The fireflies had returned to us again, their enchanting magical lights before our eyes.

. . .

Today, I welcome the precious memories of my mother. I look upon my remembrances as magical. I wait for them. And return they do. Just in a flickering I see her in my mind's eye. Just in a glimmer I catch the lilt of her voice. Just in a moment I remember the touch of her gentle hand. I wait for her magical presence. I wait for the fireflies.

...Most of all, I remember Mother. How fortunate, fortunate beyond belief, that she was my mother.

3.

~ No Place Like Home ~

IT AMAZES me that I can still see every inch of my childhood home at 1418 Carlisle Avenue even though I have not stepped inside of it for years. But there it is in vivid detail, in my mind's eye. Perhaps I can, because I loved it so.

I see the front hall with its polished banister and staircase leading to the upstairs. I see the two adjoining living rooms filled with sunshine from the big bay windows, my father's study with its wall of books packed to the ceiling, the kitchen with its flowered wallpapers and high wooden cupboards, and the dining room with its darling gateleg table at its center.

And I can clearly see our little family together within those precious walls. I am sitting in the pink striped wing chair talking to my father as he passes through the living room to check the thermostat. I am reading one of my children's books aloud to Mother in the kitchen as she prepares our supper. Perhaps I can, because I loved them so.

．　．　．

In those days of the 1950's, few people left their homes on the Avenue for long. Oh, a few grandparents wintered in Florida, sending back postcards with wondrous scenes of pink pelicans in lush gardens. My friend Carol Cook's family went way to River Falls to visit her Grandma Gregerson. And occasionally we traveled within Wisconsin to Jefferson or to Rio to visit our relatives. But most of the time we three were together at home perhaps for our own unique reason. My parents were building an accounting business, working night and day in my father's office which was located right there in that home.

So it was dramatic for me to leave home when I was nine for an entire week of summer camp located fifty distant miles away at Lake Geneva. There, in that new world, it was supremely exciting to enter the knotty pine dining hall to sit at its long gleaming wooden tables among laughing girls, even if a mixture of cooking odors hung heavily in the humid room. It was inspiring to watch the campfire at night, wearing a

CAMP AUGUSTANA FROM HILLSIDE COTTAGES · LAKE GENEVA, WISCONSIN   93130

Summer camp located fifty distant miles away at Lake Geneva

new lanyard just made in "crafts." It was fun to collect signatures in our autograph books during rest time after lunch, the quiet hour we were told that protected our lives because swimming right after eating could lead to fatal stomach cramps! Surely I would return next summer to enjoy it all over again.

. . .

Before long, it was the next summer and I was driving under the same arch with my same camp friend and her parents. But then, suddenly, without any warning, I realized that camp was the last place I wanted to be. No, there was only one place for me this year, my home at 1418 Carlisle Avenue.

My tongue felt too swollen to talk. I felt as if I weighed a ton. But I was too proud and surprised anyway to tell my friend's parents that I wanted to go home. Instead, before long their car disappeared down the road and I was stranded.

Now what was I to do? One solitary phone booth stood on the camp lawn, but making a long distance call was entirely out of my experience. A letter home would take far too long! No, instead I would go to the infirmary, a place I had taken little notice of the year before. I would explain my situation to a nurse who would call my parents and soon I would be home.

But my conversation with the nurse did not go as planned. In a cold voice I was instructed not to bother my parents. I was informed that this very week was intended to build my apparently deficient character. I was to enjoy this wonderful camp.

.   .   .

Oh, the effort it took to hide my misery! Each minute seemed an eternity, which I filled with silent prayers to speed-up the week. Only at night could I gain some measure of comfort. I would lie still in the top bunk and let the rooms of Carlisle Avenue float before my eyes. There was Mother doing dishes in the kitchen. My father was just finishing work in his office. He would be looking for me to walk to

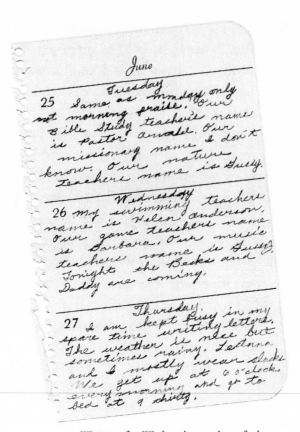

June

25 Tuesday — Same as ~~monday~~ only not morning praise. Our Bible Study teacher's name is Pastor Arnold. Our missionary name I don't know. Our nature teacher's name is Gussy.

26 Wednesday — my swimming teacher's name is Helen Anderson. Our game teacher's name is Barbara. Our music teacher's name is Gussy. Tonight the Becks and Daddy are coming.

27 Thursday — I am kept busy in my spare time writing letters. The weather is nice but sometimes rainy. LeAnna and I mostly wear slacks. We get up at 6 o'clock every morning and go to bed at 9 thirty.

Waiting for Wednesday and my father...

Marigold Dairy for a chocolate malt. Oh, there was no place like home!

Now as time stood still, I waited for Wednesday evening when parents could visit. Perhaps my father would come and I could go home with him! I hardly dared to expect him. (Mother, I knew, would not be along as she was caring for my grandmother.)

At last that night arrived, and so did my father. But the minute I saw him, something strange happened. My homesickness vanished, as did my plan to go home. The next thing I knew, a short time later my father was driving away. And just as his green 1952 Pontiac disappeared from sight, my homesickness reappeared. Now I had to endure until Saturday!

At long last, it was the final morning. Mother surprised me by coming along with my friend's parents to pick us up. What a joy to see her! We rode home in the back seat, her warm hand over mine.

By the time we arrived home at 1418 Carlisle, I was completely well. I ran through the rooms, looking lovingly at every one. Then I told Mother and my father about the longest week of my life and how glad I was to finally be home with them.

· · ·

Years later when I left 1418 Carlisle for college, thank goodness my homesickness did not return, nor did it reappear as I moved to various cities as an adult or traveled for my career.

But just when it seemed that homesickness was an isolated incident of my childhood, and I was blessed with a wonderful husband and daughter, I suffered a relapse. I was saying good-bye to 1418 Carlisle Avenue after forty-five years. It now stood empty without my loving parents. As I closed the heavy oval door a final time, those same painful symptoms appeared once again. Oh, how I longed to step inside the comfy walls to visit with them!

So ever since that day, I have come to expect the same old symptoms to strike, even just for a moment, when I still long for the comfort of that home and for my dear parents. That is when I remember what I did at camp for comfort those many years ago. I let the scenes of 1418 Carlisle float before my eyes, bringing us back together within those familiar walls.

4.

~ The Preservationist ~

DURING the forty-eight years I knew my father, I do not recall that he ever mentioned the term "preservationist." He certainly never mentioned being one. That might have required some introspection, and he was far too busy for that. He was too busy making up for lost time.

As a poor Jefferson County farm boy, he had graduated as his high school's salutatorian just when the Great Depression hit. No bookkeeping jobs were to be had. And later, World War II further delayed his plans. He was over forty when at last he became a certified public accountant finally ready to start his own accounting business.

By that time, there could not have been anyone

more fascinated with accounting, nor anyone more dedicated to providing each and every client with service of the highest quality. At the same time there could not have been anyone with higher hopes to succeed. So as my father did his best to care about Mother and me, including handing me a college education on a silver platter, he worked sixteen hour days attempting to attain personal financial security once and for all.

That left little time for other interests. And even less time for introspection.

.   .   .

However, there was one interest almost as important to him as Mother and me and accounting—our home at 1418 Carlisle Avenue, the home he and my mother had purchased on July 1, 1950, despite their fears of its $13,000 mortgage.

The old home, built at the turn of the century, was in need of repair because the original proud owner had become too aged to maintain it. But from the moment my father saw the white Dutch colonial situated on the beautiful boulevard, it was his house. Oh, my mother lived in it for thirty-five years, using her artistic talents to ingeniously decorate it. I lived in it until going away to college, and then I visited hundreds of times over the next thirty years. But all along it was really my father's house. How he loved it!

And so, although our dinner conversations were filled with accounting stories that my father could dramatically bring to life, they were also filled with lengthy discussions about the maintenance of 1418 Carlisle. And only maintenance that would preserve the home's original plan.

Inside, the original rose wool carpeting had to be protected from moths at all cost. The gleaming woodwork was forever being polished and touched-up, but never once painted! In fact, each morning, moisture was carefully wiped off of every window sill. Outside, coats of white oil paint, and only Pittsburgh Paint, were applied over and over again, even on the scalloped upper gables. Thirty storm windows were readied for puttying. New porch spindles were carved to exactly match the others and of course, the front porch floor had to be kept a dazzling shiny gray.

At times, my father performed the many tasks himself, even climbing up to the high peaks in his old age to thoroughly inspect the wooden siding's condition. Most of the time, however, he relied on others who became his fast friends. Jonas Kasperaitis from Lithuania, and the father of my friend Maria, would practically run up the gigantic wooden ladders when he painted 1418 Carlisle Avenue. Gary Larsen, our neighbor's exuberant son, took care of the lawn mowing for some years, while enlivening our quiet house

Painting 1418 Carlisle Avenue in 1950 for the first of countless times. My father would climb to the highest peak.

at the same time with his dramatic stories of teenage life. And eventually a talented person, Jon Braun, who tackled any mechanical problem, became like a son. Never did my father lose interest in preserving his house.

.   .   .

Sadly the years began to take their eventual toll on the once elegant Avenue. Greatly disturbed and saddened at the relentless changes, in his old age my father became the neighborhood guardian, attempting to preserve its past glory. He regularly paid to have debris removed from the alley. He had photographs taken of any vandalism, personally delivering the evidence to the police station.

And how he complimented residents who maintained their properties! (Although he was secretly disheartened whenever they installed manufactured siding rather than preserving the original wood.)

To move away was unthinkable, even when he was alone in the house, without Mother for the last ten years of his life. It was better to work to preserve what had once been beautiful. But to be called a "preservationist"? In his eighty's, he was still too busy to think deeply about something like that!

.   .   .

W. E. BUROW

CERTIFIED PUBLIC ACCOUNTANT

1418 CARLISLE AVENUE

RACINE, WISCONSIN

—

TELEPHONE 634-3481

5-13-95

This material was compiled by: W.E.Burow, CPA
1418 Carlisle Ave.
Racine, Wis. 53404

These sheets are intended to be of help in preparing the income tax returns
in the event the above house and any personal property items are later sold.

These sheets cover the period: 7-22-50 through 5-1-95.   Any future
transactions will have to be added to the sheets.

My father's final record of his home's maintenance for me

During the last weeks of his life, my father completed
one more task relating to his maintenance of 1418
Carlisle Avenue, about his preservation of his beloved
white Dutch colonial. Giving me a black binder titled
with that precious address, I opened it to find that it
detailed every significant project that had been done
over forty-five years on the white Dutch colonial, on
his house. It included the sad phrase, "In the event this
house needs to be sold." By compiling that final record,
he was concluding his time in his beloved home.

I was there on the day my father parted with his
house. Unable to catch his breath and needing the
care of a hospital before his death a few days later, we
walked slowly off the front porch together, marking
the end of a remarkable era.

5.

~ Next Door Neighbors ~

IN THE summer of 1950 my parents bought the only house they would ever own, a white Dutch colonial on Carlisle Avenue. That Avenue, considered a showplace in its day, stretched for what seemed a mile all the way from State Street on the south to Rapids Drive on the north. Its entire length was lined with majestic old maples and elms, furnishing luxurious summer shade from a lacy canopy above.

A wide, perfectly manicured boulevard punctuated the center of the Avenue, complete with graceful shrubbery and round milk-glass street lights. At night, their soft glow shimmered down the boulevard as far as the eye could see, as if a long strand of white pearls lay at its center. In its honor, the Avenue was often called The Boulevard.

And the imposing houses themselves, adorning each side of the Avenue, boasted two and some times three stories, with wide front porches and large picture windows. Most were still inhabited by the proud "old-guard" who had built them as long ago as fifty years before.

In 1950, Carlisle Avenue was still in its prime.

.   .   .

In that era, rarely did anyone move away from Carlisle Avenue. Grown children of the original owners simply moved upstairs to renovated flats when they married. In that way, the proud residents came to possess not only a home, but an air of superiority bestowed by their longevity on the Avenue. It was a pedigree impossible for a new family to possess.

In fact, a new family to Carlisle Avenue in 1950 often found it a lonely existence. I can still picture an elderly neighbor, "the bank president," walking home for lunch exactly at noon and then back to the bank at precisely one o'clock. Impeccably dressed in a brown suit and tan fedora and exhibiting ramrod posture, he would pass our house looking straight ahead without so much as a glance in our direction. And on Monday mornings when the neighborhood housewives hung out their wash to dry, Mother would see them enjoying friendly visits with each other across the yards while she worked alone.

It looked as if we would never be accepted by the neighborhood gentry.

.   .   .

Although the neighbors' aloofness stung, in truth, my parents were too preoccupied to make the extraordinary effort that might have led to their acceptance on the Avenue earlier than when it was to eventually occur. Married "late in life" and in their forties with a two-year old daughter when they took up residence on the boulevard, they were consumed with starting my father's accounting business. They had purchased 1418 Carlisle Avenue in part because it was large enough to accommodate his office (as was still the custom, although becoming less common, in those days) in a comfortable study they lined with books and hung with framed diplomas. There my father worked night and day to build that business.

The Dutch colonial was also large enough to convert the upstairs into an apartment. Mother herself had lived in similarly large homes when she was a teacher in Fort Atkinson. But providing the teachers with an attractively furnished apartment required considerable time on her part, as did her ingenious decorating of our entire home and the perfecting of her beautiful gardens.

And most of all, my parents never failed to take

the time to provide me with their constant love
and attention.

.   .   .

So it came as an unexpected delight when in 1952,
a young couple, Philip and Jeanette Weiler, bought the
house next door at 1422 Carlisle Avenue. From the
minute they arrived, they were friendly!

Jeanette was serene with a warm, mellow voice. A
blonde with perfectly styled short hair, she wore pretty
shirt-waist dresses, and almost always, a strand of
pearls. Philip was just a bit stocky, with dark hair and
the widest, most radiant smile. And how he loved to
laugh!

Our friendly next door neighbors were even easier
to get to know because they were often outside,
returning 1422 Carlisle Avenue to its once pristine
condition. (Just as 1418 Carlisle had been in need
of repair when my parents bought it, 1422's original
owner had also become too elderly to properly attend
to its maintenance.) Every day after Philip's work at
the J.I Case tractor plant and Jeanette's employment
in the office, they worked to transform their yard into
a beautiful park. Soon their white Dutch colonial, a
larger version of 1418, was shining with new coats of
white paint that Philip applied all the way to the high
peaks of the gabled roof.

Therefore, it wasn't long before my busy father would stop on our back sidewalk, as he went out to the garage for his car, to call over to Philip. Usually my father carried the weight of the accounting world on his shoulders, but when he allowed himself to use his dry humor, he was very clever. And Philip appreciated his wit! He eagerly listened to my father's latest pun or anecdote and would burst out laughing. Even when my father turned to accounting subjects, as he did with most people most of the time (often to my mother's and my embarrassment as listeners' attention soon dropped away), both Philip and Jeanette would listen with what seemed like rapt attention. And Mother, working late into the evenings in her own lovely gardens, would enjoy their easy conversations and appreciate their kindness. How wonderful to be next door neighbors!

.   .   .

As one year passed into the next, delightful times were spent together. There were Sunday afternoon concerts at Zoo Park, where my father played in the city band. There were a handful of summer picnics at Lake Michigan. There was the best Christmas of my childhood when Philip collaborated with my father to give me an unforgettable surprise.

And then there were our New Year's Eves at the Nelson Hotel. My parents loved the hotel's restaurant with its tall floor-to-ceiling windows looking out on Main Street, its tin ceiling, and the sparkling white linen tablecloth settings, plus the delicious roast beef! It seemed only natural to invite Philip and Jeanette to be our guests. I would go to bed early, to be awakened close to midnight. Then we five would drive downtown to enjoy a festive dinner together as the New Year began. How exciting for a child to be out in the world on such a mysterious night when one year passed in to the next!

.   .   .

Therefore, it was shocking when Philip and Jeanette broke the news to us that they were leaving. And they were not leaving 1422 Carlisle Avenue for another home in Racine. Instead, they were leaving for Mesa, Arizona! Why, such a move was practically unheard of! A few grandparents retired to Florida but we knew no one, of any age, who had left for Arizona. Philip and Jeanette had grown up in nearby Burlington and had lived in Racine for years. Now they were going two thousand miles away! For the first time we learned that Philip had long been fascinated with the West and now it beckoned to them for a new life. But we were devastated.

The neighborhood, which in the intervening years had accepted my parents and its other new residents including Philip and Jeanette, gathered for its one-

and-only potluck supper of the era to say good-bye. (My father's black and white photos of that night, with all of those dear Carlisle Avenue neighbors seated around the large outdoor table, still remain among my most precious possessions.)

The next morning, September 9, 1960, on Jeanette's birthday, we took the last Carlisle Avenue pictures of our next door neighbors when they pulled out of the alley to head West.

(Today I am embarrassed to admit that when the new next door neighbors, the Cox family, moved in, I repeated the former Carlisle Avenue tradition of rarely glancing in their direction. I was obstinately certain that no one could ever be our friends like Philip and Jeanette. And it also took too long for me to learn how very special Joe and Emelia Arnone, our other next door neighbors, would also become to us.)

.   .   .

Long distance calls in those days were relatively rare, but letter-writing was not. We learned that Philip got a job in a filling station, as it was full-service in those years. Jeanette found customer service work with Montgomery Ward. Renting a small apartment near Arizona State University and sitting under the palms on warm evenings, even without the grand Carlisle house, they felt as if they "had it made."

Philip and Jeanette leaving Carlisle Avenue for Arizona

The next important news came quickly. Philip and Jeannette were going to have a baby! We were thrilled when Tim was born, on September 26, 1961.

We had to wait a few years for a visit from Philip, Jeanette, and Tim. But one summer, we received word that they were on their way! We were ecstatic when they parked their car again on Carlisle Avenue and came up our front walk. And then we were stunned and saddened. Tim, we surmised, suffered from Down's syndrome. Mother and I caught each others' eyes during the visit, at the same time carrying-on like old times. Although we knew that Philip and Jeannette would be the most loving parents, we still felt sad for them. That day was to be our only visit with the three of them.

.   .   .

Our mutual letters continued, and of course, Christmas cards. How we missed our next door neighbors, especially on Christmas and especially on New Year's Eve at the Nelson Hotel! And so although my father continued to work long hours, frequently even on holidays, in the mid-1960's he began another New Year's Eve tradition, a midnight telephone call to Philip and Jeanette. He was always ready with a few witty jokes for them and Philip and Jeanette were ready to laugh with him, just like old times. Mother and Jeanette would enjoy their own conversation, news about Carlisle Avenue would follow, and then fond reminiscing would conclude the call. Next door neighbors were still welcoming in a new year together.

. . .

Leaving home for college in 1966 and marrying in 1970, I relied on my parents to relate news to me about Philip and Jeanette, including a heart-breaking event in 1984. Philip and Tim had been on a camping trip with other fathers and sons, when early one morning as Philip stood outside of their camper, it exploded while Tim slept inside. Philip tried desperately to rescue his son, but it was not possible to save Tim from the flames.

Now my father's New Year's Eve calls took on deeper meaning. Surely they were a gesture of genuine friendship, but perhaps they also served as a sign that at least some things stayed the same. My father made those calls until the last New Year's Eve of his life, even when he had been without Mother in the Carlisle house for most of those ten years.

When the next New Year's Eve approached, after my father's death, I could not bear to think that the calls were over. I wanted to keep the precious tradition alive even if I could not duplicate my father's humor or my mother's graciousness. I could at least call! *Really, how could I not?*

And that is how for almost another ten years we three would bring in another year together, enjoying memories of the times we all shared at the Nelson Hotel and as next door neighbors at 1418 and 1422 Carlisle Avenue.

. . .

But how fast the decades of our lives were to disappear! Suddenly my husband and I were also leaving Wisconsin. And we were leaving, in retirement, for Arizona! I would be only one hour away from Philip and Jeanette. In my mind, that made us next door neighbors again!

On my first of many visits to Jeanette in an assisted living center, I was filled with trepidation. After all, I had not seen her for forty years! Would I recognize her? What could I say about Tim? About Philip, whose memory had sadly declined, requiring care for him in another facility.

I was to find a miracle. Jeanette was still beautiful. Her blonde hair was still perfectly styled. Her clothes were still lovely and she still wore a strand of pearls, just as I remembered from Carlisle Avenue and from the very day she left for Arizona.

But most wonderful was Jeanette's gentleness, her composure, and her deep faith. Amidst a few quiet tears, she related, "Life did not turn out as I had

Jeanette and I were the two left to remember.

expected," and, "Life goes on, Carol. It does not stop for us in our sorrows." Determined to avoid bitterness, Jeanette was grateful that Tim had not suffered and relieved that Philip could no longer remember the sad days of his life.

I marveled that Jeanette, who had been our lovely next door neighbor in my childhood, was providing me decades later with a profound example of hope and strength. I was grateful that my father and mother had made the effort to keep the long-distance ties of our friendship, from the moment we first heard the shocking word "Arizona."

. . .

On my visits to Jeanette, we would turn to our remarkable memories of 1418 and 1422 Carlisle Avenue. How we missed the days when we were all together, unaware of what was to come. Jeanette and I were the two left to remember. Our eyes would shine as that life came alive for us once again: the big trees, the shining white houses, and the shimmering pearls of the boulevard lights just coming on in the evening

Why, didn't we see Philip, walking across the green lawns to greet my father with his wide smile and infectious laugh? Oh, certainly we could glimpse Mother, standing near her hedges of beautiful white and pink peonies, visiting with her lovely friend Jeanette! Surely we were all still together, still next door neighbors.

.   .   .

On one of my delightful visits to her, I was honored to receive a most special gift from Jeanette—a strand of her pearls. I treasure those precious pearls today as a beautiful reminder of her. But I also find that they serve, almost mysteriously, as a reminder of the shimmering street lights that shone like a necklace down the Boulevard that we remembered together.

6.

~ A View from the Front Porch ~

CARLISLE Avenue was a world unto itself when I was a child growing up along that grand boulevard in the 1950's. In the summer, the graceful Avenue formed a tree-lined ribbon that stretched for what seemed like a mile underneath a thick canopy of old maples and elms. At night the white milk-glass street lights on the center boulevard mixed their soft glow with the old trees, forming patterns of lacy shadows.

The homes that lined that decorative ribbon were stately masterpieces built at the turn of the century. Two or even three stories high counting some of the large attics, most were adorned with large picture windows and wide porches that looked out to view life on the sedate Avenue.

From our home at 1418, we could look far to the north to see the leafy canopy disappear into the distance until the trees and homes and street lights became a miniature creation. To the south, there were just two blocks before Carlisle Avenue met State Street, a bustling area of neighborhood specialty shops with the imposing Lincoln School dramatically punctuating the end of the boulevard. It presided over the entire final block of Carlisle Avenue with its scores of high windows and heavy doors, looking like a castle to those of us small children who would eventually attend kindergarten there.

Mother and I first walked that distance to Lincoln School when I was two or three, holding hands along the way to the "Story Hour" held there by the public library. Then I walked those blocks four times a day from kindergarten in 1952 through the sixth grade, as children went home for lunch in those days, memorizing every crack in the sidewalk and every feature of each home and its residents along the way.

In that way over the years, my mother, father, and I knew many residents to the south of us. Few people moved away and often grown children of the older residents simply moved upstairs into flats to raise their own families. Even to the north, friends and acquaintances were interspersed along the Avenue. A child's world was complete along those blocks.

. . .

The large front porches of Carlisle Avenue provided ideal vantage points to look out over the neighborhood and to view life up and down the boulevard. In the evenings, some couples sat on metal pastel-colored chairs featuring a sea-shell motif, waiting for the beautiful milk-glass street lights to go on. Older gentlemen, like Joe Arnone and John Potenziani, could be seen walking home from the local Italian lodge, the gentle light from the milk-glass globes slightly illuminating them, with only their cigar tips piercing the dark. Children's voices would be heard as they roamed the neighborhood playing Tag or Hide-and-Go-Seek until familiar grown-up voices were heard calling them in.

During the days, mothers in flowery house dresses would stand out on the porches to visit with the mail-man, or the newspaper boy, or to greet their children coming home from school. Young children could watch the few cars go up and down the long Avenue when they spread their dolls or trucks out on the porches to play or to make tents from blankets hung over ropes tied between the railings.

Our front porch had a wide, shiny, wooden, gray floor, railings with scores of carved spindles, and tall columns with Grecian-looking scrolls at the tops and bottoms, all painted in glossy white. A visitor would have to first walk up five steps from the street to the top of the sloping front lawn, and then another five wide steps of the front porch to reach the big oval leaded glass front door. The lawn's height gave the house at 1418, as well as those like it on the same side of the block, just a bit more prominence.

.　.　.

Our front porch received the most attention from my father. Oh, he was far too busy building his accounting business to sit on it on a summer evening. That never happened once in the forty-five years he lived at 1418 Carlisle. But it was a frequent subject at our dinner table, if there was time left over after his accounting stories of the day, told dramatically to Mother and to me. My father watched every inch of that front porch with an eagle eye to keep it in perfect condition. Under his direction, it was frequently being scraped and hand-painted, swept or washed.

Like my father, my mother, too, was over-worked. Married at forty-two and then a new mother at forty-four, living in a large home with flower gardens that she loved but that demanded her time, attending to the teachers who lived upstairs, helping in my father's business, and devoting herself to us, she seldom could enjoy the front porch either.

So I became the only one in our little family to

actually use it. Mother encouraged me to play there with my dolls and books and neighborhood friends, often helping me to get "set up." Before long, she would bring us graham crackers covered with chocolate frosting. In those days, my father, usually in the greatest hurry as he went between his office and his business appointments, would stop to joke with us in his own unique way. Sometimes he would ask us to pose out on the lawn, taking black and white photos that live on today as my priceless treasures.

. . .

Oh how quickly those childhood years were to disappear, leaving just their idyllic memory behind! I would no longer be taking my familiar walk to Lincoln School, but I would be going north and then east to Washington Junior High and later north and west to Horlick High School. Although I loved Mother and my father beyond description, the importance of life on Carlisle Avenue began to quickly recede in lieu of teenage dreams, crushes, and more complicated school work. I had a new and larger world than Carlisle Avenue to encounter!

That is why I was unconcerned with the new neighbors who moved in next door. Why, I was thirteen and far too busy with my emerging teenage life to think about Mr. and Mrs. Cox and their small children! In my heart, there could be no one, anyway, to replace Philip and Jeanette Weiler, whom I had thoroughly loved since childhood and who had sadly left for Mesa, Arizona. I fully accepted the custom in this old neighborhood, that a home would remain "titled" in the former owner's name for years afterward. I agreed that the Cox family was really living in the Weiler house and it was the Weiler's I still thought of.

But Mother began to talk more and more of the lovely family next door. Having been a dedicated teacher for many years before marrying my father, she loved children and they loved her in return. The little Cox children began to visit her out in her gardens, or they would knock on the back door calling out her name to come to talk with them. In the kindest of ways Mother would teach them about birds and trees and flowers, all of which represented her deep faith. Carlisle Avenue was the world of those children now!

. . .

On some pleasant afternoons during a few of those teen years in summer and into fall, Mother would gently suggest that I sit on our front porch once again, this time to read to the oldest Cox child, Colleen, from the hundreds of children's books stored throughout our old Carlisle house. Colleen was an adorable child, tall with curly soft brown hair, large serious brown

Colleen on the steps of 1418 Carlisle Avenue

eyes, and high intelligence. But I was torn! There were evening plans to make! An important telephone call might come for me that I would not want to miss.

But Mother's kind manner was very hard to ignore. Deep down I knew that I wanted to be like her, to be as caring as she was. So occasionally I would spot

Colleen running between our houses and call to invite her over to the porch for a brief time. She would come immediately and we would sit together on the porch steps, reading a favorite book or two.

As we read, we also had a view from the porch of life on our Avenue. There would be Mrs. Barden's piano students arriving at her front door directly across the street and then the sounds of their lessons being played, for better or for worse. Mr. Washburn would be getting out of his little black Ford that he took back and forth to the popular A & W Root Beer stand the family owned. Joe Arnone would be perfecting his front lawn next door to the south so that not one blade of grass was out of place. Children would cruise down the long sidewalks on their bicycles waving up at us.

As the stories came to an end, my thoughts would have already turned to my late afternoon and evening plans with my friends. In my heart I was glad that I had responded to Mother's fine values. I had enjoyed myself to an extent, but I simply could not devote another minute to a neighborhood child! We would close the last book, Colleen would scamper off, and I would promptly set-out to Racine's North Beach or to watch a game at Horlick Athletic Field. Maybe that same night I would walk home under the Carlisle street lights with a handsome ball player, to be dropped off at that very front porch.

.　　.　　.

Looking back now, those teenage years were to van-
ish just as quickly as had the days of childhood. Before
long I would return to Carlisle Avenue only as a visitor.
I would eventually learn from Mother that the Cox
family had moved to another area of Racine. She was
becoming too frail to go out visiting, and so it was only
through Christmas cards that my parents remained in
touch with the family.

When my mother, and then my father, were unable
to continue writing those cards, I used Mother's
address book to make sure that my parents' holiday
greetings were still sent out. And it only seemed natural that when my parents were no longer here, I kept
up the tradition, sending one to "Mr. and Mrs. Cox
and Family." After all, the Christmas cards had gone
back and forth for decades.

Each year I found a great deal of comfort to recognize Lorraine Cox's handwriting once again and to
know that some aspects of life still seemed to remain
the same. Our mutual messages were brief, but often
there was a delightful picture included from Mrs. Cox.
(How could "the children" now be in their thirties?
And how was it possible that the youngsters I viewed
were not Colleen, Marie, Tricia, Jack or Joe, but their
children?) I had not seen any of them since my college
days were over.

．　　．　　．

It was the Christmas of 2000 that my greeting cards were difficult to write. That year I had been diagnosed with a serious illness and my prognosis was uncertain. I enclosed this information with my cards.

Not long afterward, in February when I was at a low point in my life, a letter arrived with an unfamiliar return address: Oak Park, Illinois. It was from Colleen. Reaching across the decades, her letter was filled with words of love and encouragement, with words of a deep faith. There were fond childhood recollections of visiting with Mother in her garden. There was Colleen's most beautiful remembrance of her, bringing tears to my eyes, when she described Mother as the "Saint Francis of Carlisle Avenue." And there was a vivid picture of my father, always in business suit, white shirt, tie, and hat, taking a moment to talk and joke with the neighbor children.

Then there was her most special recollection of the two of us sitting together on the front porch of 1418 Carlisle Avenue, reading and looking out upon our Avenue. I learned with astonishment that those brief times, when an older girl read to a child on a late afternoon, had become a life-long gift to Colleen. I was instantly appreciative that Mother's guidance had once again proven to be so wise.

Of course I had to call her! My heart was full of

gratitude for her memories. We laughed and cried and a new friendship was immediately ours, no longer affected in the least by an age difference. I was easily in awe of her, a person of the keenest intelligence, the deepest faith, with a warm voice and delightful humor, committed to her mother, her siblings and their families as well as to her many friends.

I had no trouble forgiving her when Colleen confessed to "spying" in fascination on the older girl who left on dates, departed for a high school prom, and who provided the excitement of a wedding right next door. And I listened in wonder to her own favorite stories of the world she experienced on Carlisle Avenue.

.   .   .

Now Colleen has returned to live in Racine. I, too, return regularly to our hometown. We meet and reminisce and laugh and cry, sitting in my condominium living room with much of the furniture from the grand old Carlisle home around us. We have found that we are soul-mates, with so much to share from our past on the Avenue and so much to look forward to. I remember her father painting the big house next door on bright summer days. I remember her grandparents coming and going, all of them gone now. I delight in hearing about all of the Cox children and their children, and about Lorraine, the mother of this magnificent family.

It is amazing to me that Colleen and I both cherish the memory of the view from the front porch, of the old neighborhood and its precious people. It is even more amazing to me that we share a similar view of life today.

Colleen has her own home today, a charming bungalow. Its front porch is warm and inviting. It is perfect for her. It is perfect for us. We sit on it together, looking out upon her Avenue.

7.

~ When Television Came to Carlisle Avenue ~

THERE was once a street that seemed to stay the same forever. In fact, if you had gone in search of that street in the 1950's and if you had walked for what seemed like a mile along a beautiful boulevard called Carlisle Avenue on a summer day, you may have agreed that this was just the place that never was going to change. A sense of permanence permeated its blocks.

You would have noticed the stately homes that lined the Avenue with their high peaks and gables, standing in place just as their proud owners had built them at the turn of the century. Huge old maples and elms would have graciously leaned down casting thick shade from overhead. And friendly mothers, wearing flowered house dresses, would have stood on the grand front porches, visiting with the neighborhood children.

A caption for this idyllic scene could have read, "Here Time Stands Still." I can see it all now in exquisite detail because this is where I grew up, at 1418 Carlisle Avenue.

But then, unexpectedly, change arrived after all, even though it was barely noticeable at first. If you had looked more closely on your next walk, you would have observed a large delivery truck pull up to a particular home. You would have seen men carefully maneuver a huge box into that house. In a few hours, you would have noticed the same men high above, anchoring a huge metal contraption to the once stately roof. And if you had returned to the Avenue in the evening and passed in front of that house, you would have observed that a greenish glow had replaced the golden light that would have once shone out to the boulevard from its living room.

Television had come to Carlisle Avenue. But it had not come to one home, the one at 1418.

·   ·   ·

As the Avenue changed, so did I. As more and

more antennas went up, my spirits went down! Even at age eight, I understood that my parents would never believe in television. As kind and as generous as they were to me, they simply would not believe in wasting time watching a black and white box. Both of them had worked too hard for too long to feel carefree enough for that.

Why, my father had ploughed farm fields with teams of horses in Jefferson County from the time he was a child. He had walked four miles into high school on dirt roads. Then he had worked long years to obtain his accounting education in Chicago, sometimes going without enough money to buy food. Now he and my mother worked night and day right in our home to build their accounting business.

As for my mother, her father's sudden death when she was only three had left the family in precarious straights. Working from a little girl on, she had nevertheless gone away to college in the 1920's. For nearly the next twenty years she had conscientiously dedicated herself to teaching until she married my father "late in life."

On top of that, I knew, too, that both of my parents believed in reading, not in watching. No matter how tired my mother seemed at the end of the day, she always found time to read wonderful books to me like *The Moffats, The Five Little Peppers* and countless others. Even I had to wonder how we could read if we were watching television.

With my heart sinking even further, I knew that my parents simply didn't like change anyway. Why, it took my father years of deliberation to buy a car! Now in 1955, we had a beautiful two-tone green 1952 Pontiac, but we also had a black 1938 Chevrolet with running boards!

While I longed to be watching programs like *Howdy Doody* and *The Lone Ranger* like everyone else on the Avenue and everyone else in my third grade class, I said very little to my parents. I knew it was hopeless.

. . .

So I was thrilled when my parents let me accept my friend Jackie's invitation to watch *Disneyland* with her family every Wednesday night. The Olsons' lived in the upstairs flat just two houses down at 1410 Carlisle Avenue. What should have seemed a very short walk over, though, sometimes seemed to take forever. Mysterious shadows danced all around me when the glow from the milk-glass street lights filtered through the dark swaying branches. Even the Olsons' deserted back hall with its creaking wooden staircase took forever to climb. But the dark walk was worth it when I took my place on the floor with Jackie's family crowded in to the little living room to watch Tinker

Bell float across the screen. Walt Disney himself would speak right to us, telling us how glad he was that we were watching. It was completely exciting!

. . .

To this day I cannot fully explain what happened soon afterward on a spring Saturday when my father and I had made one of our frequent trips to his little hometown of Jefferson. After stopping at Main Street's Milky Way Restaurant for our usual hamburger and rich chocolate malt, my father surprisingly did not walk back to our parked car. Instead he took a few steps in the opposite direction, turning directly into the narrow store front of the Jefferson Radio & TV Clinic. While I listened in disbelief, my father said the astonishing words, "I think it's time that we bought a television."

In shock, I held my breath, hoping against hope that the store's owner would prove to be an expert salesman. My father was certain to have so many detailed questions that I feared their discussion would actually lead to ending his new idea. Amazingly, one by one the questions were answered with the utmost seriousness. In fact, before long the owner was offering to drive the sixty-five miles to our home in order to personally analyze our television needs.

It was agonizing to wait the few days for his visit,

as I continued to worry that my parents would change their minds. But I realized that my father, especially, must have deliberated a very long time before he turned to a trusted hometown friend to make his monumental purchase.

That is why in due time a delivery truck pulled up to our house and a big Zenith television set was maneuvered into our living room. And that is why, not an antenna, but an enormous TV tower was cemented into the ground and erected into the sky on the advice of the Jefferson Radio & TV Clinic. Change had amazingly come to 1418 Carlisle Avenue.

. . .

More amazing to me was what followed *after* the delivery. Certainly my parents were apprehensive about their child growing up in a culture different from their own. However, I was allowed to watch our new television freely from the start. Even more amazing was that given the permission to watch, I still took the opportunity to read. Mother's love of books had had its lasting influence and we continued to read together most nights. When my third grade teacher Mrs. Hudson read aloud the brand new book *Charlotte's Web* to our class, I was enthralled with Charlotte and Wilbur, reading my own copy over and over again. Mary Poppins arrived in my life via her umbrella, as did

A huge TV tower was erected.

detective Nancy Drew in her fashionable convertible. No doubt I would have read more without a television, however I don't think that I missed many wonderful books either.

In addition, my household chores seemed to go faster than before. After all, I had countless new families to become acquainted with when I was finished! There were the Nelson's, the Anderson's, the Cleaver's and the Stone's. Curling up to watch in our comfy old pink-and-white striped wing chair, I loved the treats Mother would surprise me with: apples or oranges, her chocolate frosted graham crackers, Cracker Jack or Red Dot potato chips.

There was also the Wild West to learn about with Roy Rogers and Dale Evans, Annie Oakley, Wild Bill Hickok and Jingles, the Lone Ranger and Tonto. On Friday nights I could solve crimes with the handsome private eyes on *77 Sunset Strip*. I could laugh out loud at the hilarious neighbors Ralph and Alice Kramden and Trixie and Ed Norton, or at Lucy and Ricky Ricardo with their neighbors Ethel and Fred Mertz. I could be part of the Mickey Mouse Club and learn to act like Annette. And although watching Ed Sullivan on Sunday evenings was sad because my carefree weekend was ending, there was nothing as exciting as seeing Elvis on that stage!

.　.　.

Only occasionally did Mother join me, and how I loved it when she did! I knew that she was torn because there was always more work for her to do in the house, in her gardens, preparing her Sunday School lessons, and in the business. Try as she might, though, she simply could not resist *I Remember Mama*, about a mother from Norway, just as her own had been. Her work definitely stopped, however, whenever there was a Billy Graham crusade!

My father, on the other hand, was never once to watch that Zenith, or any other television in the many years that followed at 1418 Carlisle Avenue. Never did he lecture Mother or me, never did he find fault with us. He simply continued to work, which he had learned to do so effectively as a farm boy. Most likely his life was filled with more drama than any television program could provide anyway. He was completely fascinated with accounting, with IRS audits to ward off for worried clients, with detective work finding a suspected embezzler, and with the suspense of meeting relentless tax deadlines. He would walk through the living room to check the thermostat or the weather outside, and would visit with me a little, but he would never watch our television. Somehow I understood, even though at times I pictured the Olson family nearby at 1410 all watching together.

Only in his eighties, when my father was frail and living alone and would come to visit my own little family for a few days, did he take a glance at our television. Most of the time he kept his old familiar briefcase nearby in case he would have the strength to open it and study one more fascinating accounting topic.

Today, how I wish that I could thank my father and

mother for taking a chance on change! Time revealed that their risky decision proved to be a good one. Not only did that Zenith and enormous TV tower give me a lifetime of memories of wonderful television, when television was wonderful, it gave me a lifetime example of a little family trying to understand and do its best for each other.

8.

~ The 1400 Block ~

MY CHILDHOOD was spent in a vast and fascinating place. Stretching all the way from Albert Street to Kewaunee, it included huge trees, large lawns, and flower gardens of lilacs and peonies. Gleaming cars of the 1950's occasionally traveled by. And there was an array of old two-story houses, each with intriguing residents to know. This enormous place was the 1400 block of Carlisle Avenue.

At its center was our side, the "even side" of the block. We called it the even side because all twelve houses had an even-numbered address, including ours at 1418. They formed such a lengthy row that it was only from our upstairs airing porch that I could look down to see them all at once. But then again, we children

MY HEART LEADS ME HOME

could easily skip down the sidewalks to see what was going on. Seldom did anyone move away, and so each resident and every house became an important fixture in this world.

Far across, way on the other side of the Avenue's beautiful boulevard, was the odd-numbered side of Carlisle's1400 block. But the eleven houses that faced us (plus one vacant lot) were so far away that we came to know those residents mainly by watching their interesting comings and goings from our front porches.

(And if that were not enough, the 1400 block of Summit Avenue was just behind us across the alley. There stood the backs of eleven more houses with their wide grassy yards ready for us to play on.)

With so many houses and yards and residents, I knew that I lived in a fascinating place.

.   .   .

But even at a young age, I knew that life in our house at 1418 was different. Our family of three seemed far more serious than anyone else on the block.

Perhaps it was because my parents were older than the others. Perhaps it was because there were only three of us. Maybe it was because my conscientious father was building his accounting business from his office right in our house. And perhaps it was that my mother had been a dedicated teacher (she still taught Sunday

School), who loved to quietly read books and write letters when her house and garden work was done. I whole-heartedly loved my parents, but sometimes it was tempting to wonder what a livelier, more carefree house might be like.

. . .

So it was not a surprise when Mrs. Larsen from down the block at 1434 Carlisle called about her son Gary. He was having trouble with his fourth grade math. Would Mother tutor him? Soon Gary arrived one night a week to sit at our gateleg dining room table, close to my father's office. With such an intriguing development in our house, as a younger child, I "hung around" to watch.

However, as great a teacher as Mother was, her pupil suffered—from acute boredom. The hour not only included Gary reciting multiplication facts, it included a variety of sounds at loud volumes. The sounds were Gary's impressive imitation of trucks, motorcycles, and fast cars, all things that he found far more intriguing.

While Mother tried to keep Gary's attention, another person was noticing. My father, from his office, was unable to ignore the combination of mathematics and vehicle sounds. Always a serious student himself, he wanted this young boy to learn. However, he could appreciate Gary's dilemma. With such a passion for

My father was listening from his office...

vehicles, Gary was hard-pressed to focus on multiplication. My father's heart was won over.

Now he assumed a role in Gary's tutoring by teasingly "egging him on." But just as much attention was given to Gary's imitations of this sound or that as to mathematics. My father would shake his head and laugh. Their bond was forged.

With Gary's next report card, the mathematics crisis ended. And so did the tutoring.

But not Gary's visits. Often on nights when he walked his black Labrador, Jet, a loud knock would be heard at our back door. In he would bound to describe some antics of the day. Of course they were exaggerated, but Gary could make any story exciting. His smile and his laugh penetrated our serious lives and our quiet house.

.   .   .

When a teen, Gary continued to share more interests with my father. One was car shopping. While the Larsen family frequently bought Fords, resulting in Gary driving up and down the Avenue in a yellow and white Fairlane (with a girl right beside him on the bench seat), my father deliberated for years before buying. Gary never tired of studying endless specifications with my father and planning strategies to use for yet another meeting with one more dealer.

Another became "Larsen, Incorporated." Gary expertly took over our car washing and waxing, snow shoveling, and lawn mowing. But my accountant father insisted that Gary prepare legible and accurate bills before "the corporation" could be paid. Such details were of little significance to Gary, but he laughingly attempted to comply.

Once after "Larsen, Incorporated" mowed our lawn, a new adventure occurred to Gary. Stealthily climbing our immense TV tower, he jumped over to the upstairs porch, quietly walked through the second floor, and suddenly appeared in our kitchen. Gary had accurately envisioned the shock he would achieve, but not my mother's reaction. My sedate mother ordered him to immediately leave the way he had come. Then, as he left, we all laughed.

As his teen years continued, so did Gary's stories. There were the "Adventures at Sea," as Gary had enthusiastically discovered fishing and boating on Lake Michigan with his dad. And there were the tales of high school life, the Horlick High cafeteria pranks, looking for "chicks" at the city's Main Library, the revving of engines and "scooping the loop" downtown on Friday nights. I wondered how a serious student like me could survive when I got there!

. . .

Years later when I finally entered high school at Horlick, I found it surprisingly calm and orderly! And coincidentally, I found it amazing that the vast 1400 block of Carlisle Avenue was growing smaller. When I went away to college and later married, it was even stranger that the 1400 block had almost disappeared. It was only 1418 that I really noticed when I visited my precious, serious parents. Many of the oldest residents were missing, as were my great childhood friends, including Gary.

Then my own parents were sadly missing from the block and it was time to sort through forty-five years

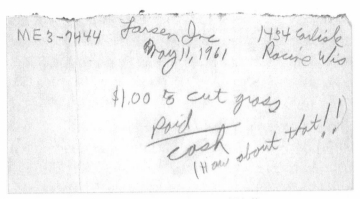

A "Larsen, Incorporated" bill

of sentimental treasures. Black and white photos of my childhood friends, taken so carefully and dated by my meticulous father, were there. And so were the "Larsen, Incorporated" bills, carefully saved in his "strong box." How I hoped to renew my old friendships, including those with Gary and his wife Jane!

Not coincidentally, the 1400 block was now enlarging. In fact, I could suddenly picture the entire row of twelve houses in minute detail and envision every former resident.

Gary and Jane, whose father was our beloved Lincoln School principal Mr. Temme, had moved to Florida, to Naples, where the boating and fishing begun in Racine could continue. But when Gary returned the next time to Racine for an annual Lake Michigan fishing tournament, we got together. That day I parted with just some of my father's "Larsen, Incorporated" bills.

.   .   .

Today, when I return to the block of my childhood, it is a vast and fascinating place. Of course I linger at 1418, almost, but not quite, catching a glimpse of my dear parents. I enter every one of the yards. I stop in at every one of the other eleven houses, and I silently greet each former resident.

In my mind, I thank each and every one for the contributions they made to my life. Among them, I thank Gary for shedding his light on a very serious little family and giving us the precious gift of fun and laughter over many, many years.

9.

~ Walking Through My World ~

WE WALKED everywhere when we grew up in Racine in the 1950's and '60's. We started on our own block before we were school age, walking over to the houses of our friends to call for them. I often walked a few houses down to see my friend's doll house, the biggest in the world, complete with electricity.

By junior high, it was nothing to walk from Carlisle Avenue to North Beach for the afternoon or even to walk all the way across town to Washington Park Pool. My friend Linda Benedict Rannow recalls a walk that lasted an entire day, taking her from High Street to Lincoln Park and home again. Winter did not stop us. On cold clear nights we walked to the zoo for ice skating under the glowing lights.

In high school, I would walk home late at night all the way down Carlisle from Rapids Drive, watching the shadows dance between the leaves and the lights on the boulevard. Across town, others in West Racine were walking home just as the North Shore gave out its final whistle for the night.

. . .

By the time I was seven, I knew the world of my neighborhood like the back of my hand. I knew the world between my house at 1418 Carlisle and Willie Quadracci's store two blocks away on Albert Street. I had walked there many times for Mother, often with an extra note written at the bottom of her grocery list, "Willie, please let Carol pick out a treat today." I can see myself peering down into the rectangular freezer, trying to decide between a fudgesicle or a root beer popsicle for the walk home. I knew the walk to Albert and State Park, where we gathered in the pavilion's shady breezeway on hot summer afternoons making lanyards with the park recreation leader.

But most of all, I knew the world of Carlisle Avenue between my house at 1418 and my grade school— Lincoln—which stood at the end of the boulevard. I had first walked to Lincoln hand-in-hand with Mother when I was three, to the public library's story hour held there.

Beginning in kindergarten, I had walked down

Lincoln School still looking like a castle today

Carlisle to school, making two round trips a day because we walked home for lunch in those days. Some times we walked in groups or in pairs or some times I walked alone. In that way I knew which sidewalks were tilted and cracked. I knew that when a sidewalk was replaced it would bear the mysterious name stamped into the concrete, "John J. Johnson." I knew which houses looked most inviting. I knew which were the shadiest sections with the biggest trees. And I always looked across the boulevard to my nice piano teacher's house, Mrs. Anderson's. This was my world

.   .   .

On my walk to the first day of second grade, I thought that the two previous school years had prepared me to know the world I would find *within* Lincoln School. Our friendly principal and school secretary, Mr. Temme and Miss Nelson, would greet us from their office door. The supply room would be open, smelling of crayons and fresh paper. The pictures of Lincoln and Washington, Boy Blue, and the West would be hanging in their places. And all of my old classmates would be back.

But nothing prepared me for the surprise that awaited us in our classroom. There, already seated, was a NEW GIRL. Why, having a new girl was rare because seldom did anyone move in or out of our school. We learned that her name was Andrea Richardson and she had come to Racine all the way from New Jersey. (Most of us had never met anyone from as far away as New Jersey.) I watched Andrea smile at us, seeming to be so friendly and at ease. I immediately admired her!

Even more surprising as the fall weeks wore on was that Andrea Richardson seemed to especially like me. Me, of all people! Why, maybe I wasn't too serious after all. Maybe I wasn't too tall or awkward, even though I towered above every one of my classmates except for Billy Weber. And maybe being an "only child" didn't make everyone assume I was spoiled. I was grateful for the friends I had grown up with, but sometimes I wondered if they thought I was too serious. It was thrilling to have the new girl like me!

So when Andrea brought a note from her mother to mine, inviting me to walk home with her for lunch the next Wednesday, I could hardly wait! And it is that very walk home for lunch that remains in my mind today.

. . .

Andrea led us across State Street to Haas Drug Store and then down to Lincoln Super Market. We turned on Prospect Street, right into a fascinating new neighborhood world. First of all, we walked uphill. (Why, Carlisle Avenue was completely flat!) Intriguing little side streets jutted here and there into Prospect in topsy-turvy fashion. Houses of all sizes and shapes stood at the curbs or were situated behind others, completely different from the lengthy straight line of sturdy Carlisle houses with the boulevard running right down the center. If that weren't surprise enough, before long we arrived at a three-story yellow brick building, looking silent and scary. Here stood a mystery right on a neighborhood street!

But more was to come. Next to the mysterious brick building was a thick woods protruding right on to the sidewalk. There, barely visible through the leaves, was a black metal railing that secretly marked the top of a hidden cement staircase. Holding on to the black railing, Andrea led us down, down, down, perhaps a

The mysterious stairway

hundred steps amidst the overhanging branches. At the bottom, we emerged in sunlight to see the Root River and a footbridge leading to a pretty white house. Andrea's house.

. . .

Mrs. Richardson, looking very dressed-up, greeted us in a mellow voice and with a friendly smile. We three sat in a cozy kitchen, visiting easily together. As we talked, Andrea's mother served us something that I had never heard of before, let alone eaten before, Welsh Rarebit. I thought of my own mother and knew she would be proud of me as I remembered to secretly say a

Andrea's house

little table prayer and to profusely thank the hostess for the delicious lunch. Trying very hard to be a perfect guest, I did not tell Mrs. Richardson the truth, that I could hardly swallow the rich Welsh Rarebit.

All too soon it was time to walk back to school. But I was no longer the same child who had walked to Andrea's one brief hour before. Like other children who were learning about new worlds as they walked throughout Racine in those years, in that short time I had encountered an astonishing new one, with new people and new places. On that amazing walk, I had entered a new world on the road to growing up.

·   ·   ·

There were to be more walks and more lunches that year. But before long, Andrea Richardson was to move away. We intended to be pen pals forever, but lost touch in time. Today, I wish that I could thank Andrea for her friendship and for the day I first walked home for lunch with her. I would explain that such a positive childhood experience did, in fact, help to set my life pattern for meeting new people and exploring new places. (And perhaps I would tell her that I never became taller than 5'4 ½" and that I was untruthful about the Welsh Rarebit!)

Today when I retrace that walk, the mysterious building and the footbridge are gone. But I can still find the hidden staircase and Andrea's house still stands near the river. And whenever I hear "New Jersey," I think, "Andrea Richardson lived there."

· · ·

Following the newspaper publication of this story, a reader contacted Andrea Richardson. Since then I have had the greatest pleasure in reliving this day with her!

10.

~ Porch Lights ~

SUDDENLY it was impossible to concentrate on coloring our maps of the forty-eight states. Just a few minutes earlier, it had been fun to trade crayons with each other for more colors. But now something much more exciting was happening, and right outside our second grade's tall Lincoln School windows. It was impossible to keep our eyes from straying to the scene outside. Why, a fantastic snow was falling!

It seemed like it was going to take forever to be excused to the cloak room, to line up single-file, and finally to escape out the double doors. Because nothing could compare to walking home in brand new snow!

We were going to jump right into it, make snow angels, and stick our tongues out to catch the snowflakes.

Boys' snowballs would fly through the air! In fact, walking home to my house on Carlisle Avenue was going to go too fast!

. . .

Reaching our homes, we could barely sit at our kitchen tables long enough to devour the snacks our mothers had waiting, even if for me it was chocolate milk and windmill cookies. Then we waited impatiently for mothers to check the clips on our mittens or untangle the strings connecting them through our jacket sleeves, tie our scarves tighter over our heads and mouths or fasten our caps. At last we would be out the door until supper, barely hearing their voices calling after us, "Don't get too cold!"

How lucky to live on the even side of Carlisle Avenue's 1400 block, as Jackie Olson, Gary Larsen and I did, because our front lawns had an actual hill! Everyone brought their Red Flyer sleds received directly from Santa Claus or picked out from amazing displays at hardware stores like Mohr Jones downtown, Kortendick's on State Street, or Thrifty Mac on Lathrop.

Or how lucky to live on the 1400 block of Summit Avenue behind us, like Carol, Sharon and Billy Cook or Martha, Peter and Steve Rocque. Their backyards were huge open snowy spaces that we covered before long with snowmen, tunnels, and forts.

Only when we heard the distant rumble of a snow plough did we stop to watch its enormous headlights pierce the dusky evening and to see it tossing big bundles of snow onto the curbs, making mountains for us to walk on.

Oh, there was nothing like playing outside in a snow storm!

But then, hard as it was to leave our snowy adventures, there was nothing like seeing the front porch lights on for us. When we stepped into a warm back hall, it felt so good to be home. And supper smelled so good!

.   .   .

Some times after supper we went outside again, perhaps to walk on our skates to Albert and State Park. Or on Reschke Avenue nearby, Pat Ingrasci and her friends were playing exciting night games of "Cut-the Pie." With her driveway and front lawn covered in snow, the conditions were ready for stomping out a huge circle for the "pie," "cutting" it into four sections, and then beginning a wild game of tag.

When the snowy night finally ended, mothers checked us for the slightest signs of a "runny nose," a cold or a cough, treating us with their remedies of cough syrup made by neighborhood druggists, golden Luden's and Smith Brothers' black or wild cherry cough drops, and with their treatment of choice, layers of Vicks lathered on us.

With our mittens drying on the heat registers and snow pants and jackets hanging on basement clotheslines, we were ready for the next day.

.　.　.

On many of those winter nights after supper, though, I stayed inside. Oh, I could feel torn, thinking what fun my friends were having together outside. But it was just so comfy to sit next to the heat register in our pink wing chair, cutting out paper snowflakes and reading my library books. It was just so nice to visit with Mother, to have warm Ovaltine together, or Hershey's cocoa made from scratch. Every so often my father would leave his accounting work to talk with us as he checked the winter scene out of the front windows. How good the love and security felt to me in that old living room!

.　.　.

In just a few more winters, however, the familiar snowy activities of our neighborhood blocks changed in favor of far bolder adventures. The Carlisle front hill now was for babies! Instead we went sledding to the big hills of McKinley, North Beach, Shoop, and Lincoln Park. Albert and State Park was far too tame for ice skating in comparison to the zoo, which even had a warming house, although it was located right below the pungent animal floor.

To my dismay, however, the new heights were more scary than exciting for me. As the hills got higher, so did my fears, until finally I suffered from a worrisome dilemma. Certainly not wanting to be thought of as a "scaredy cat" or spoiled only child, I resorted to a new strategy: lies. *White* lies, all filled with phony excuses of why I could not meet with my friends. When I did go along to the big white hills, fun as it could turn out to be, I still relied on a few secret prayers to get me safely down.

Never once, though, did I go down Racine's greatest winter wonder, Washington Park's famed toboggan slide. The concrete, iced chute was known far and wide to provide the most daring, frightening ride. With a park employee giving a push at the top to the toboggan teetering over the edge, there could be no turning back! How I wish that I had dared it just once, before the colossal landmark ended as part of Racine's winter history.

. . .

Thank goodness that when I looked out of Washington Junior High's tall windows at an afternoon snowfall, I was not the least fearful! I knew that a snowy walk with my girlfriends would be on *flat* sidewalks, even if we were going for miles in the cold all the way Downtown, perhaps to the YWCA, Zahn's

Department Store, or to Kewpee's for a hamburger and malt. Of course, we would not be caught dead in snow pants and for some, even the leggings we wore when leaving for school in the morning were stored in nearby bushes for the day. No scarf ever covered our hair-sprayed heads! After all, who knew when and where we might find boys? With our jackets left stylishly open, little did our mothers know how cold we became!

Likewise, both mothers and fathers would have been shocked if they had seen their sons "skitching" on the rear bumpers of unsuspecting drivers after school, holding on to the cars for dear life, breathing in the exhaust fumes. From Washington Junior High, they passed us going all the way up High Street to Carlisle.

.   .   .

And then suddenly we were in high school with brand new adventures once again. The family car was now our prime interest. We begged to use it, never letting on that we accidently fish-tailed the rear-wheel-drive vehicle on glare ice or that we drove way too soon before the slow-working defrost uncovered the icy windows.

But on those wintry evenings, our porch lights would be on for us, and even if we went right to our rooms in typical "cool" teenage fashion, we were home.

Supper still smelled so good! And maybe, down deep, we appreciated that mothers seemed overly-concerned about us and that dads had already shoveled the walks.

. . .

Looking back today, I can see that as we children ventured out into the world seeking winter's adventures, it was only a preface to facing the adventures of *life* that we were to encounter, with its joys and challenges (and with its fears). Just as loving parents welcomed us in to safety for the night and prepared us for the next day, we are still as much in need of the precious kindness of those who wait for us today.

And so when I occasionally drive past 1418 Carlisle Avenue on a winter's day, the home that I left long ago now, I look up at its little hill to the bay window. I imagine that my father is looking out from that front window to check the snow, ready to start shoveling for us. I envision my mother walking through the front hall, putting the porch light on for me.

And when our grown daughter comes home to visit us, I leave the porch light on for her.

11.

~ Mother, Mary, and Me ~

IT WAS a delicious sort of early Saturday morning, when the temperature was just the right sort of hot, when big leaves of summer hung over our house on Carlisle Avenue, and shadows formed lacy patterns on the front porch as the sun filtered around the fancy spindles.

Coming down the stairs from my bedroom to join Mother for breakfast, I stopped for a moment at our front door to look out on the porch and our block. All was quiet, but soon piano students would be heard from Mrs. Barden's across the street. Neighborhood children would be riding down the sidewalks on their bikes. The colorful cars of the 1950's would be passing by.

I looked out at Mrs. Barden's across the street.

It was a delicious feeling to sit with Mother in our old kitchen, enjoying toast piled high with butter, cinnamon and sugar. (And perhaps my father, already out on errands, would soon bring us "bismarks" from Lincoln Bakery.) It was a perfect morning.

. . .

Well, almost a perfect morning. Because one troublesome thought hung silently in the air. SCHOOL! It was about to start. And with it, so were my worries. Even though my years at Lincoln School had gone fine, here I was again, worried about the final one, the sixth grade. Anxious thoughts kept intruding on the perfect morning. *Would I get good grades? Would my teacher be nice? Would I have my old friends? Would I get even taller?*

While both of my parents urged me to be less conscientious, Mother especially empathized with my predicament. Many years before, when she was Miss Ann Fadness, she had been a favorite junior high school teacher in Fort Atkinson. I knew as we sat together in the kitchen that she understood me.

And then, just during those quiet moments on that early morning, our doorbell suddenly rang. While Mother went to answer it, I stayed in the kitchen to savor not only our delicious cinnamon toast, but one of the last mornings of summer.

. . .

It took a long time for Mother to return. When she did, she came with surprising news. The conversation with the stranger at the door had brought her back to the first years of owning our white Dutch colonial, and even before that to the years she had lived in Fort Atkinson.

You see, my parents had been frightened to buy our home in 1950 with its huge $13,000 mortgage! After all, they were just starting my father's accounting business. But the formal dining room could be converted to his office.

And the upstairs, already with a kitchen, could become an apartment rented to teachers. Why, when Mother had lived in Fort Atkinson, she and other teachers had rented rooms in large old homes. Now perhaps my mother could follow that same example.

Soon the apartment was listed with Racine's Superintendent of Schools and every fall, two new teachers arrived to rent it. Mother, of course, loved the chance to visit with them about teaching. But for a young girl, having "the teachers" upstairs was completely fascinating! They would leave for school in stylish suits or pretty shirtwaist dresses with matching jewelry, nylons, and even high heels. Their hairstyles and make-up looked perfect, as were their polished nails!

And after school, it was pleasant to faintly hear them quietly moving about upstairs or listening to their radio or record player. Occasionally we overheard them in the front hall making a rare call on the one telephone in our house. And how exciting for me to be invited upstairs for supper as their guest!

(Today it is wonderful to recall those days with Dorothy Blotz, one of those delightful teachers! I love to hear her fondly recall the cozy apartment upstairs and the kind invitations from my mother to come downstairs to visit over ice cream.)

. . .

In time, however, my parents decided to keep 1418 Carlisle just for ourselves. The apartment was closed with its kitchen and bedroom left untouched. Its living room, though, became my bedroom. On hot summer nights, its windows would be wide open for the breeze, giving me a view of the hushed Avenue below, with the milk-glass street lights glimmering through the lacy maple leaves.

.   .   .

But then, on that summer morning when I had come down from that very bedroom and Mother and I were sitting together in our kitchen, a new teacher to Racine was the person ringing our doorbell, intending to ask about our apartment for rent. Mother, kindly explaining that it had been closed for some time, felt badly that the inquirer, Mary, had somehow received an outdated rental list. Wishing her well, Mother and I resumed our own precious morning.

It was early evening when the doorbell rang again. There stood Mary asking if Mother would reconsider. She had so enjoyed their morning conversation! Really, a living room was unnecessary! Sharing the upstairs with the family's daughter was fine! And it was just for one school year, as she was being married the next June. It was *this* home that Mary wanted.

Within a surprisingly short time, because of my

mother's wise and generous nature, our family's unexpected decision was made. Mary was to come.

.   .   .

At first, Mary and I seldom saw each other, keeping our bedroom doors closed. I was getting used to the harder sixth grade school work. Sometimes on Indian summer evenings, my friends and I would walk for miles, or Mother and I would read and visit until late. Of course my worries about the school year remained obstinately present.

Gradually, however, Mary and I began to spend time together. Before long, we were walking to Lincoln Super Market for her groceries on Saturday mornings. Occasionally we took the Red Line downtown on Friday nights to walk through Zahn's Department Store and to leisurely browse at Martha Merrill's Book Store, ending our shopping with fudge from Fanny Farmer's pretty corner shop. Mary invited me for an unforgettable night at Racine's community theater to see *Arsenic and Old Lace*. We were finding a great deal to enjoy together!

Soon it was dawning on the three of us that Mary was one of the most special people we would ever meet. Tiny and darling, with a radiant smile and lilting laugh, she was also brave and determined. She had already studied abroad! And she was extremely intellectual, listening to opera on her record player and reading right through the dinner hour, holding a book in her left hand while she ate with the other.

As we became friends, it was not my hope to be intellectual like Mary. But I *was* beginning to hope for the same pleasure she had in simply being herself. I was thinking that it might just be possible to believe more in myself. In fact, I was already worrying a bit less.

. . .

However, a new worry was emerging, not a worry about a first day of school, but a worry about the last. Mother and I were already predicting how badly we would feel when it was time for Mary to leave us on the last day. And then Mary eliminated those worries in the most surprising way. I was to be her junior bridesmaid! That would give us more time together and how thrilling it would be!

We shared the most exciting spring, corresponding with the dress-maker, having high heels dyed to match (even though I would tower over the bride!) and planning my stay at Mary's home during the wedding week.

I left ahead of my parents on the Greyhound, acting as grown-up as I could for the week's festivities: a luncheon in a neighbor's pretty dining room (an occasion that remains my standard for social events to this day), gatherings with Mary's fascinating friends who had returned from places as far-off as Europe, pleasant conversations in her darling Cape Cod home "run" by her capable grandmother and mother since her father's untimely death, and, of course, meeting her fiancé.

The wedding took place on a perfect summer day.

.   .   .

With that special summer's end, the apartment was closed once more, never to be rented again. When I walked through the empty rooms, they were silent, but in fact they resounded with priceless memories of Mary and our wonderful year. Mother and I sat together once again in the old kitchen on those last precious summer mornings, enjoying delicious cinnamon toast and our wonderful talks.

We knew that I was worried about going on to junior high school. *Would I fit in? Would my subjects be awfully hard at Washington? How would I find all of those rooms, especially one that was numbered 400?*

But we both sensed that my worries were less than the summer before. Having Mary as a friend and role model had indeed changed me. My world was larger and my confidence higher.

An astonishing turning point had occurred, just at

the right time for a young girl entering the new world of junior high school.

Perhaps that was what my wise and loving mother had secretly hoped for from the very beginning.

.   .   .

Today, author Mary Gardner and I remain in touch. How I appreciate the opportunity to tell her what she has meant in my life!

12.

~ In Style ~

AT ONE time my mother was extremely stylish. Long
before I was born, black and white snapshots pictured
her in style, wearing darling flowered dresses and high
heels, posing with her classes when she was a teacher
in the 1930's and '40's. There were photos of a 1945
summer day when she and my father celebrated their
engagement. At forty-two, she was tiny and wearing
an adorable ruffled print dress. I loved to look at her
in all of them.

And even in our linen closet at 1418 Carlisle
Avenue, faded Gimbel's dress boxes storing hats and
gloves still lined the shelves as evidence of her past pur-
chases. Certainly without a great deal of money, but
as an artist, my mother had ingeniously created her
stylish flare.

Mother in the 1930's and 1940's

But for most of us children growing up in our 1950's Carlisle neighborhood, no matter how in style our mothers might once have been, they no longer seemed overly interested in that subject. And they looked fine to us! Like most, my mother wore practical "house dresses" and even went out on the front porch occasionally with her hair in curlers.

It seemed entirely natural that our mothers looked like, well, like mothers! What we noticed was their love and attention, like waiting for us with peanut butter and jelly sandwiches when we walked home for lunch every day from Lincoln School. And we, as their young daughters, were not particularly interested in style either, running through backyards wearing faded pedal pushers with our hair flying out behind us.

.   .   .

Until we changed in 1960, the year we became teenagers. Suddenly we were interested in style. Very interested! We were part of the new and amazing world of junior high school, where excitement and anticipation seemed to literally hang in the air. *(Why, in just two minutes when the bell rang, who might walk us to our next class?)* It was important to be in style to look our best, to be ready for the next important event that might be just around the corner!

Actually, we were not alone. The entire country was

enthralled with the style of the new President's glamorous wife Jackie Kennedy. *Life* featured her at the White House and at a place called Hyannis Port. We longed to be taller, to be thinner, to have thicker hair, and to have a personal dress designer like Oleg Cassini. But since we could not, instead we slowly paged through *Seventeen* and *Glamour*.

And we relied on TV commercials, especially for just the right beauty products to buy. Our hair styles (the "flip," the "bee hive," and the "bubble") demanded the greatest time and attention, and the most products. From Breck and Prell shampoos to Toni home permanents, rollers, portable hairdryers, "rat tail" combs, and cans and cans of extra-hold hairspray, we bought them all. For our complexions, we depleted entire jars of Noxema, overlooking its antiseptic nose-stinging aroma. And as we lay out in the sun for hours, we covered ourselves with Copper Tone and Johnson & Johnson baby oil to achieve the promised golden tan.

American Bandstand was another reliable source for style, regardless if it came from distant Philadelphia. As we secretly danced along in front of our living room televisions, we decided on our next outfits to buy. Shopping for hours at Eitel's and Zahn's, Levin's, Kay Campbell's, Penney's and Goldblatt's, we bought mohair sweaters, pleated skirts and sweater sets, and matching knee socks. We selected nylons from walls of thin boxes at Nu-Mode Hosiery. The hours worked after school as lunch counter waitresses, Zayre's clerks, and babysitters of rambunctious children were entirely worth what we earned for style.

(Perhaps at the very same time, our male classmates were watching TV commercials and programs to *enhance their* own style, like noticing Edd Byrnes as Gerald Lloyd "Kookie" Kookson on *77 Sunset Strip* continuously combing his hair. Aromas of Vitalis, English Leather, Brut and Aqua Velva could fill a car, just as our My Sin by Lanvin or Wind Song by Prince Matchabelli did.)

.   .   .

And then we waited, hopefully for the next exciting event, best if tinged with a hint of romance, but just as often followed by keen disappointment. On Friday nights we went to Y dances where we did the twist and the stroll and hoped that the someone we had in mind would take us home. On Sunday afternoons, we sat near the encyclopedias at the Main Library, hoping that that someone would walk by to work on a report.

Summers, especially, were filled with anticipation and excitement. Who might we "run into" on the 4th of July or at the North Beach? Who might be walking into the sweltering Nitty Gritty club or the Ivanhoe

on a particular night? We needed to be continuou
in style!

.   .   .

However, as much as we had come to understand
style, thoroughly studying it for six years from 1960
to 1966, it was often our mothers we could not
understand. They had been young once and in style,
but now they frequently did not seem to fully grasp
how important style was to us. They did not seem to
understand how much time it took to perfect our "hair
do's" or why we needed to be on the family phone
so long. They worried that we might be "boy crazy."
In concerned tones, mothers reminded us about our
grades, our goals, and our inner values. Deep down,
we both longed to understand each other!

Amazingly, my own mother remained exceptionally
calm and understanding despite her concerns for me.
Old enough to be my grandmother, she still seemed to
well remember her own youthful desire to be in style,
even though long ago she had turned to higher goals
of inner beauty. In turn, I especially wanted to thank
and please her by making the honor roll, planning to
attend her college, and following her faith. But there
were still times when I rolled up my pleated skirt to
make it shorter after I walked out the door.

.   .   .

sly

g of 1966, we were struck with the
he six special years begun in 1960
an end. And we realized that possibly
ing it, we had changed again. We had
re serious after all, and perhaps we had
me a bit like our mothers! Astoundingly,
thought about missing them as plans to leave
merging for college and for jobs and for moving
from home.

Although most of us would never again have the
ime or as innocent a world to think so often about
being in style, there was one last supremely stylish
event to anticipate before graduation. PROM. Suddenly
I realized that I wanted my mother, and only my
mother, to go with me to pick-out my dress. We went
to the Ruth Carnes shop on Sixth Street and selected
a floor-length pink A-line, which I thought had the
exact look of Jackie Kennedy.

On Prom night, when couples arrived at Memorial
Hall to a fanfare of onlookers, there were crinolines
and colors and corsages and hair styles and jewelry
of all kinds. That night was the apex of our high
school style. For hours, we danced to the great songs
of the sixties and as it ended, I will never forget the
bittersweet moments as we watched the sun rise over
Lake Michigan. Our high school days were over. Life
had inevitably moved us on to a new era that was about
to dawn.

. . .

Today, that pink prom dress resides in its own tissue-lined box, right beside other faded dress boxes I still keep containing a collection of my mother's lovely fashions. The boxes and their contents are just one precious reminder, among countless others, of us as mother and daughter. Regardless of the decades gone by, what remains forever in style is the love we had for each other.

13.

~ Cooking Class ~

BY THE time my mother finally married at age forty-two, she had gained twenty years of experience as a teacher. In fact, she was so loved as a teacher in the 1930's and 1940's that I still hear from some of her students. But in all of those forty-two years before she married, my mother had gained virtually no experience as a cook.

In those days, a single teacher usually took a room in a large home where meals were provided. For years my mother stayed at Mrs. Menzel's on Whitewater Avenue in Fort Atkinson, joining the other female boarders each evening for dinner served in the large dining room. Even when my mother met my father in his hometown of Jefferson, it was in the dining room of the Jefferson House where both of them were boarding.

Though she had worked hard as a child to help her own widowed mother, my mother had not been required to cook. While her mother became an accomplished baker and sold her famous rolls to make ends meet, my mother helped with the washing and ironing, cleaning, and sewing. When there was time left over, it was for studying to keep up her high grades, taking painting lessons, or exploring the woods on her bicycle.

In time, her sister Ingeborg married Ben, and her brother Andrew married Elva, and my mother became a frequent guest in their homes. But she was not asked to cook.

.   .   .

So when Mother became engaged, the exciting news spread quickly. Why, who would have thought that Miss Ann Fadness, at her age, would marry? And the groom himself had seemed to be a confirmed bachelor! It was so exciting that well-wishers sent more shower and wedding gifts than usual, including an entire collection of colorful Fiesta dishes. There were silver casseroles and fancy candlesticks. Mother carefully placed the elaborate white and cream tablecloths and napkins she received in her "hope chest" to be ready for the pleasant future luncheons and dinners she was sure to host.

Of course, Mother was presented with a copy of the new cookbook, *The Joy of Cooking*.

Fortuitously, the ladies' auxiliary of Rio Redeemer Lutheran Church was also just putting out a cookbook filled with recipes from their venerable cooks. All of these gifts Mother brought to Racine to the newly-weds' tiny apartment on Ashland Avenue and later, in 1950 to 1418 Carlisle Avenue.

In that dear old Carlisle kitchen I remember so well with its high wooden cupboards and its flowered wallpaper, setting the table was something my mother could do with a flare. After all, she was an artist! She could arrange the various Fiesta colors, tablecloths and napkins in the most wonderful combinations, adding flower arrangements from her beautiful gardens. She could arrange the food with ease to look like it came from the kitchen of the Waldorf Astoria.

It was only the cooking of that food that presented a problem for Mother.

.   .   .

No one could have wanted to please her family more than Mother. And no one could have complained less. But in that precious old kitchen, my father and I silently understood that every meal presented a grave challenge to her. For one thing, Mother was tired by the end of the day. Here she was at age fifty with a kindergartener, my father's accounting business to help with, a large home to clean, and laundry to do in the basement with her wringer washing machine.

And then, even though she never seemed quite ready to admit it, there were so many more interesting things to do than cook, like taking just ten minutes here and there to read the *American Home* magazine for decorating ideas, or to write a letter to Ing or Elva, or to perfect her exquisite gardens. A neighbor child might be calling at the back door for her, or it was time to prepare the lesson for her Sunday School class. Most of all she was always ready to talk with me, read with me, encourage me and compliment me in any way that she could.

On top of that, Mother was a perfectionist. She had earned an "A" in teaching, and she could even understand taxes to help my father. But she had a fear of failure in the kitchen. Deep down, she doubted that her cooking efforts would measure up to her high standards. One day, but not today, she would try some of the hundreds of recipes she was collecting.

Most of the new recipes were from Ing, who carefully wrote them down as she listened to experienced farm cooks slowly read their favorites on the Jefferson County radio stations. And both Elva and Ing would faithfully send handwritten recipes copied after tasting a delicious torte at a Ladies' Aid Society meeting in Jefferson or Rio. Plus in those days magazines were coming out with amazing new inventions such as ingenious Jello combinations, quick casseroles, and countless cake mix variations. Mother continued to plan her imaginary meals.

.　.　.

As I grew up, my mother *did* slowly but surely perfect a handful of recipes for our little family's evening meals. And they were delicious! Oh, how I wish that I could be seated this very night at that old kitchen table with my dear parents, with the attractive dishes and napkins, as well as the food that was really so appealing. (Of course we never began until Mother read the daily devotion to my father and me because that was of prime importance to her.)

Some of her standards became "Mrs. Sundby's Chicken," named for the wife of Rio Redeemer's venerated minister. She even tackled "boiled dinners" with ham or spareribs steaming in a pressure cooker that sounded dangerously close to exploding.

Her favorite desserts were delectable. In summer we relished her strawberry shortcake made from Bisquick, taken warm out of the oven, smothered with butter and covered with fresh strawberries delivered to our

P. 45

Date Torte — From Granny's Bk.

1 c sugar   1 egg (beaten)
2 T butter   1 c pitted dates (not chopped
    Pour 1 c boiling water over dates
    + dissolve 1 t soda in mixture.
1¼ to 1½ c flour   1 t vanilla
½ t salt   nutmeats (optional

Directions : Pour 1 c boil. water over dates +
    add soda. Let stand + cool while
    mixing other ingredients. Blend sugar
    + butter well; add beaten egg - mix well.
    sift flour, salt + ½ t B.P. together
    + add to butter mixture. Lastly -
    add dates + do final quick mixing.

Mother's favorite dessert recipe, which she mastered.

back door from Lincoln Super Market. "Date Torte" was her finest dessert, dark and rich in taste, with just the right amount of whipped cream on top. There were often warm oatmeal cookies waiting for me after school, or delicious strips of her home-made pie crust sprinkled with sugar, as well as an apple or rhubarb pie itself.

I am so glad that my father and I recognized her efforts and generously complimented her. How could we not, since she never failed to encourage *us*?

.   .   .

But as Mother's confidence increased for "regular" meals, it did not increase for special ones. Cooking for company remained quite frightful. Cooking a full-scale holiday meal was even more cause for alarm. And nothing was as fearful as cooking a turkey for Thanksgiving.

Before every holiday, letters (because long-distance telephone calls were rare in those days) would go back and forth about which family would host that special day. Each time Mother waited in suspense. She worried endlessly about cooking any holiday meal, but she hoped beyond hope that Thanksgiving would not fall to her.

Eventually a satisfying pattern emerged. We would almost always host the Easter holiday dinner. Mother would serve a ham dinner with scalloped potatoes, applesauce, Catherine Clark's Brown and Serve rolls, and her delicious date torte.

Elva and Andrew usually hosted Christmas in Rio, at the home where the three siblings had grown up at 504 Lincoln Avenue. How Mother, and all of us, admired Elva's ability to bring the most wonderful dinner to

I can still taste another of Mother's favorites.

that dining room table in what seemed an effortless manner. She would serve "Grandma Fadness's rolls" from the old family recipe which even required yeast!

Thank goodness that Thanksgiving then fell to Ben and Ing. Ben had been a butcher at one time and had even worked at a meat packing plant. He actually *enjoyed* preparing a turkey and its dressing. Mother, spared from her fears once again, would secretly vow to try a Thanksgiving dinner the next year when she was sure to be ready.

In this way, for the forty-five years of her married life, Mother never did prepare a Thanksgiving turkey. I know that in her heart she always imagined that she would be ready the next year. Instead kind relatives understood her fear and intervened. We knew how much she loved us and we loved her without question in return.

. . .

On Thanksgiving weekend in 1970, I married my husband John in our hometown of Racine. Like my mother, I brought little cooking experience to my marriage. And like my mother, I found that I was only too glad to be a guest for many Thanksgivings to follow.

But when I became a mother myself ten years later to our daughter Lisa, an unexpected change occurred within me. I experienced a different kind of love as a mother with a new sense of responsibility. And I experienced a new appreciation for my own mother. I wanted to live a life that did credit to her memory as her daughter, thinking of myself as her representative.

That is why I eventually felt ready to cook my first Thanksgiving dinner, turkey and all. I had my mother's blue and white *Joy of Cooking* to help me. I had my own wedding gift, a bright orange edition of *Betty Crocker*. Best of all, I had her as my silent partner. It felt as if we were helping each other, together in our own special cooking class. Remembering how my mother had never failed to generously praise and encourage me, I could smile as I knew that she would be so pleased that I was continuing on where she had left off.

So on any Thanksgiving I am ready and willing to cook for my wonderful family and friends. Oh, I suffer some anxiety, but I resolutely set the table with a beautiful old-fashioned tablecloth. I use a few favorite pieces of Fiesta. I plan a table prayer. And then I wait, with a bit of trepidation, for the food to be done.

My husband and our daughter wait with me—and yes, I believe, my mother waits with me too.

Section II

~ AWAY TO THE COUNTRY ~

Gently they go, the beautiful, the kind;
Quietly they go, the intelligent, the witty, the brave.
I know. But I do not approve. And I am not resigned.

~Edna St. Vincent Millay

14.

~ Summer Road Trips ~

WHEN summer arrived and our Lincoln School stood strangely silent, we gravitated to Albert and State Park for perfect long summer days of the 1950's. There we did "crafts" in the shady pavilion, played serious marbles, and almost wore out the old metal slides and swings.

In the evenings we gathered on the big lawns belonging to the new houses in the 1400 block of Summit, just across the alley from the stately old two-stories on Carlisle Avenue where I lived. There, uninterrupted by such inconvenient things as fences or garages that came afterwards, we joined for Hide-and-Go-Seek, Red Rover, Tag, or simply running around helter-skelter. Only when our names rang out as our mothers called us in, or when the street lights came on, did we turn to home.

We knew every kid in the neighborhood and mentally took attendance as if we were back in our Lincoln classrooms. After all, hardly anyone left the neighborhood for long. Therefore, it helped to explain an upcoming absence by calling out as an evening ended, "Tomorrow night I'm going to Kiddie Land," or "Tomorrow we're going to The Beach." No further explanations were needed, as we were well acquainted with Racine's fantastic attractions. For instance, "The Beach" meant only one thing, the amazing mile-long stretch of sand along Lake Michigan. The same under-standing applied to "The Zoo," or to "The Outdoor." Just mentioning three words, "Washington Park Pool," conjured up identical images of that impressive outdoor swimming structure, looking like it came right out of a 1930's Hollywood movie set.

A few destinations we called out were a bit farther away and consequently less familiar to most of us. I figured that Brown's Lake was that very color until I saw it years later when I finally got to Burlington thirty miles away.

Some of the destinations were so far away that only our imaginations could fill in the gaps. "We're going to my grandma's!" was one of those. We knew that Carol Cook's Grandma Gregerson lived in a distant place, River Falls. (I still imagine a white gingerbread-style house situated close to a pleasant water fall.) Jackie Olson's family left every summer for an obscure destination: "Up North." Their little Nash Rambler nearly touched the ground with camping supplies and all five Olsons inside. To this day, Jackie is not quite certain where "Up North" actually was.

In my neighborhood, I don't remember anyone calling out a distant destination like California or Florida. Airplane travel was not in our consciousness. Most of our car trips, long as they seemed, were confined to Wisconsin, if not Racine County itself.

.   .   .

Because school was out, parents decided that it was time for summer road trips together in our family cars. If we had a car. And not everyone did. Amelia and Joe Arnone next door did not have one. Why should they? Joe could walk to work at Belle City and all of Amelia's sisters lived right over on Blake Avenue. With their son Louis in the Navy, a car was unnecessary.

Besides, friends would proudly share theirs. Rosemarie Hurlimann Romano's parents didn't own a car because they worked continually in their popular High Street bakery. But one summer, friends drove them all the way to Wisconsin Dells for its famed attraction, a boat ride down the Wisconsin River, topped by a black Labrador dog's breathtaking leap into mid-air between two high rock towers. If we were not planning a trip to Mount Rushmore, we had our own amazing Wisconsin rock formations to visit.

Some rides led to lifetime religious results. Linda Schubert is a Presbyterian today because her family received Sunday rides to church from the two families they lived between. Both families were Presbyterian.

．　．　．

Sometimes the hours cooped up together in our cars passed quickly. Sometimes they stood still. On winding and hilly two-lane roads, we might be stalled behind a slow, invisible object like a farm tractor far ahead. On every Main Street we might be stopped for a train of one hundred cars. It was only natural to bombard our parents with, "Are we almost there?"

Because time in the car could take forever, we attempted to claim a favorite position.

Caye Putning Christensen preferred the ledge behind the rear seat, where she could stretch out underneath the back window on the way to Washington Island.

Parents tried to help pass the time suggesting novel games like counting barns and horses, and reciting state capitols. Arlene Niesen LoPiccolo's beloved grandmother encouraged her passengers to recite the rosary. Occasionally we stealthily kicked each other or conducted silent pillow fights. Some parents understandably chain smoked the entire way.

It was hot, but in actuality, we had simply traded a hot house for a hot car. Jackie Denning Stern, growing up years later and whose family did drive to the West, still remembers being attached to the hot plastic seat covers on August trips to Las Vegas.

For relief, we pulled into country waysides for our peanut butter and jelly sandwiches and Kool-Aid laced with sugar. Just occasionally, we stopped when a rare A&W Root Beer stand came in to sight.

.   .   .

At the end of some evenings, I would call out, "We're going to Jefferson!" That small city sixty-five miles away became associated with my family just as River Falls belonged to the Cooks. My father had never forgotten his hometown, despite leaving it for his accounting training in Chicago and then settling in Racine. My parents had even met in Jefferson, when Mother arrived to supervise teachers of the country schools. Not only were there plenty of heartwarming visits to make with relatives and friends but there were clients to meet, as rarely did my parents ever feel they could be completely on vacation.

But no matter how often my father said that he was

"pressed for time" in his business, that did not apply to his driving. He was the slowest driver anyone could imagine. If other families thought their summer car trips seemed to take forever, they had not driven with him. Mother and I knew that my father's driving speed did not matter at all in the big scheme of things, but when a long string of cars piled up behind us on our way to Jefferson, it was embarrassing!

Perhaps my father had disliked speed since he was a boy driving a team of farm horses that got away. Never had he forgotten the "Runaway." Perhaps it was the Great Depression that made him frugal in many ways, except when it came to providing wardrobes of clothes for me and countless books for Mother. Driving slowly saved the brakes, the tires, and maybe the entire car. (He would keep a favorite car or two for decades.) Mother and I never learned exactly why he drove so slowly and in all those years, we never found the right time to ask.

In those days, our family even owned two cars. One was a two-tone green 1952 Pontiac. The other, a testimonial to my father's ability to save a car, was a big black 1938 Chevrolet, complete with huge head-lamps and running boards. Mechanically sound and immaculate though it was, this old car clearly drew further attention to us. It was finally replaced in 1958 by a very long Chevy Bel-Air, in a bright aqua color

The two-tone green 1952 Pontiac

Mother and I with the big black 1938 Chevrolet

The aqua 1958 Bel-Air finally replaced the 1938 Chevrolet

that actually seemed completely out of character for my conservative parent.

Just getting down the alley out to Albert Street at two miles an hour was the lengthy start to our trip. Reaching Waterford seemed to take a day. But then something wonderful would set in as we slowly drove our familiar route on the back roads. The further we traveled away from Racine and the closer we came to Jefferson, the more our cares lifted, the more we three talked and laughed.

. . .

By the time we arrived at the Milky Way Restaurant for our hamburgers and malts, we may as well have arrived in Disneyland. The city's setting, still so vivid in my mind today as it looked then, would have rivaled any magic kingdom. There, the ornate Jefferson County Court House, with its clock tower high over head, presided in stately fashion from the city square. Huge elms and maples formed thick green canopies over the streets, with pillared mansions interspersed underneath. Modest frame homes glistened with fresh paint and bright flower gardens. And all were surrounded by bright red barns, white farm houses, green fields of high corn, and pastures dotted with grazing black and white cows.

We loved seeing friends and relatives, and even the clients, all of whom seemed to treat us like celebrities. My mother had been everyone's favorite teacher! My father had taken part in the best boyhood pranks: "Remember the hay wagon perched on top of the school roof?" At the Burow family farm, originally owned by my grandparents, Aunt Virginia and Uncle "Bun" would warmly greet us and there would be a brief time for me to roam the yards and pastures with my cousins. Then too soon the day would be ending and we would be driving slowly, oh so slowly, toward home with the light from the Court House clock tower growing dim in the distance. Together in our car, we three would feel a special closeness after such a perfect day.

The next evening I would be back on the big lawns of Summit Avenue just like everyone else, almost as if I had never left.

. . .

When Lincoln School's doors opened for us again in the fall, we thought that our summer road trips had ended. Little did we guess that those trips were not really over, but that we would fondly take them again and again in memory. They were to last a lifetime.

In fact, each summer I drive my parents' winding route from Racine to Jefferson, appreciating any reminder of the car trips we took together so long ago. In truth, I would give almost anything to have just one more trip with them again. I would even ask my father to slow down, so that I could savor every precious moment and mile.

15.

~ Summer Magic
with
Aunt Virginia ~

WHEN the bright and shining Wisconsin summers of childhood have vanished, one by one and year by year, it is time to turn to magic: the magic of our memories to keep those precious summer days alive forever. It is time to see again in our mind's eye the bright blue sky, the green grass and the corn as tall as a house. It is time to sip the best malted milk in the world, to catch the biggest fish from the river's edge, and it is time to feel the delightful absence of school. The magic can indeed make those precious moments and those childhood summers last a lifetime.

Cousin Lynn, Grandpa Burow, and Uncle Bun on the tractors, with Aunt Virginia, cousins Sandy, Jimmy, Kenny, and me

Remembering the idyllic summers of my childhood over fifty years ago brings me magically in an instant to a farm on Highway 89 just outside of Jefferson, the Burow farm. Here my father's brother Elroy (nick-named "Bun" years before) and his wife Virginia ran the family farm once owned by my grandparents. And it was here that my uncle Bun and my aunt Virginia enthusiastically welcomed me, the studious, gangly, "city slicker" whom my parents had brought from our home sixty-five miles away so that I could play with my country cousins. In those years, Robert wasn't born yet, Lynn was already too old for our antics, but Kenny, Jimmy, Sandy and I found endless adventures together!

We would roam about the farm yard with its many out-buildings, checking the chicken coop, the pig pen, the corn crib, the shed and the garage. We would sneak into the dark, still barn to spy on the mean bull and then climb into the high hay loft. We would play with the farm dogs, the cats and the kittens. One day in the woods, Sandy and I stumbled into deep mud that transformed my new citified penny loafers into heavy black blocks!

Once in a great while, a lone car would come down the road, and we would run out to watch it go by. Once in awhile, a friend or relative would stop, and we would hang around listening to the grown-ups talk out on the lawn.

At noon, we would sit at the round oak table in the kitchen, eating Aunt Virginia's delicious mounds of mashed potatoes, stacks of chicken along with home-made pickles and fresh tomatoes from the garden. We would listen in awe to Uncle Bun talk about the crops and the field work with the men who helped him. Would it rain? What tractor needed repairing? What did the WGN radio noon farm report from Chicago say about the price of milk? The men were lean and tan, laughing and smiling, undaunted by their work on a blistering hot summer day.

When they pushed back their chairs and left the table for the fields, we children would also leave to find the next adventure that was surely waiting for us.

Aunt Virginia in her farm kitchen

· · ·

Many years later, and long after Uncle Bun had passed away, I had the honor of speaking at my aunt Virginia's funeral service. It was time to remember the great gifts she gave to us when we were children on the farm, although none of us cousins could have ever really forgotten. I fondly recalled the sentimental picture:

Let me paint the picture that is in my mind today. It is a country scene, a hot summer day. The sky is bright blue with an occasional billowy cloud. The farm yard and buildings are surrounded by fields of tall corn, grown to an astonishing height. The bright red barn is cool and dark inside, very quiet except for the rustle of a few dark-eyed horses and the occasional stomp of the restless bull. Cows are grazing peacefully down near the woods.

When my parents and I arrive, we see Uncle Bun far in the distance out in the fields. When he comes in to greet us, he is "tall, dark, and handsome" with a deep tan and a huge smile. Aunt Virginia comes out onto the lawn from the white farm house. We stand under the big leafy shade trees together.

Idyllic? Of course! But such is the miracle of childhood memories.

My parents and I have come from Racine in our 1952 two-tone green Pontiac. There is not a question in my mind as I stand on the lawn about the rest of the day. It will be filled with adventures! My cousins and I will play everywhere: in the farm yard, the barn, out in the woods and the pasture, mud and all. I am happy to be here. I am wanted here! (And I know that on other days, more cousins will visit here, having just as carefree a time.)

The memory is so simple but so powerful!

Today those of us children from that era are already far older than Bun and Virginia were in those days. We can more fully appreciate what Aunt Virginia gave to us. Placed on the family farm, she could have been a shade unwelcoming, a shade too busy or too critical of us. Instead, she welcomed all of us, as did her children, with open arms. She allowed and fostered joyous experiences of young cousins together.

Who knew then which childhood moments would become indelibly etched in our minds to last forever? Did Aunt Virginia guess that the vision of those days would stay with us? Because she did indeed give us youngsters a life-long gift. We remember being welcome, being loved and being children together shielded from every care in the world.

Of course we learned that those days could not last forever. There would be joys and many sorrows to follow. But the farm memories remained an anchor. And truthfully, all of the years I visited Aunt Virginia afterward when she lived on Fischer Avenue in Jefferson, it only seemed a temporary residence to me. There was a feeling that soon she would go back and we could all resume our times together on the farm.

Now we believe that Virginia has been taken to her

true home. But she has left us with precious memories and heartfelt appreciation.

. . .

Today I must visit my aunt Virginia, my uncle Bun, cousin Lynn, and cousin Kenny, as well as my own dear parents at a far different destination than the farm, the Evergreen Cemetery in Fort Atkinson. That beautiful place soothes any sadness I may feel when I visit.

I do not go past the farm any longer, as it looks far different from the days when the tiny white house and bright red barn glistened in the sun, when children played on the manicured lawn, and when a herd of black and white cows grazed down by the woods. Sandy and I still find places to meet, though, and laugh when we recall my muddy shoes as if it all happened yesterday.

However, it is ever so much easier and more pleasant to visit by letting my magical memories float before my eyes. Why, my childhood summers have not vanished! I have kept the summer magic. There we are together on the farm once again. The sky is blue, the corn is high, and we are laughing together once again around the big kitchen table.

16.

~ Our Guests From the West ~

TODAY I went back to the Burow farm just outside of Jefferson for another grand summer reunion, just as I had done when I was a child. In fact, I went back in June and I plan to go again this July and perhaps in August. Because, you see, I will be there in memory.

How I love to picture all of us together once again! My cousins and I are still in our youth, the adults are still in the prime of life, we still have the same red barn and white farm house as our familiar setting, and our relatives Aunt Mildred and Uncle Ted are still our guests of honor. When I keep my vivid memories before my eyes, *we are* together again. Neither the intervening years nor those same reunion guests have vanished.

On reunion days, I would be up early, excited to make our trip out to Jefferson from Racine. Although the drive always gave my parents and me a special time to visit with each other, frankly, on reunion days it gave us too much time. The trip seemed to take us forever! Even though my father was always "pressed for time" due to the demands of his successful accounting business, he simply would never drive over forty-five miles an hour.

And his slow driving made it a foregone conclusion that we would not take the "fast roads" that were coming in. Instead, we would wind over our familiar route through Waterford, Mukwonago, Eagle, Palmyra and finally into Jefferson. Even when the farm's red barn, with its striking white doors, came into view across the fields, it still seemed to take us too long to get there!

. . .

I knew just what the reunion day would be like: the temperature would be ninety, the sky a perfect blue, the corn surrounding the farm a fantastic height. I was certain to be welcomed by my cousins on the farm, the children of Aunt Virginia and Uncle Bun, who ran the farm in my grandfather's place. Kenny, Jimmy, and Sandy would be ready to share their adventures with me, even if I was their serious cousin from the city. And there would be more cousins from other Burow families

The relatives gather in front of Uncle Ted's and Aunt Mildred's car.
Back row: Grandpa Burow, Uncle Ted, Aunt Mildred,
Mother, Uncle Bun. Second row: Cousin Lynn,
Aunt Virginia. I am in front with Cousin Kenny (hiding).
Our 1938 Chevrolet is in the background.

to join us as we roamed the farm in carefree fashion. We could have been on the grounds of a grand estate.

I knew that when we arrived, my mother would join my aunts in the farm kitchen for almost the entire day. They would spend hours preparing the delicious potato salads, pickles, watermelon, rolls, corn, casseroles, and baked chicken. They would serve delicious cakes topped with thick frostings. Finally it would take them hours to wash, dry and put away the dishes. Never once were they to run out of conversation. Only if a child needed them would the aunts stop.

Uncle Bun might hurriedly be finishing some field work and toward evening some of the uncles might help him with the milking chores. But during most of the day, the men held continual games of horseshoes out on the front lawn. All of us, aunts and cousins alike, loved to hear their hearty laughter across the yard and the clinking of metal on metal. Only when card games started up in the farm kitchen later in the evening did our little family depart for home, as "cards" were not an interest of my parents and work was always waiting for them there. The drive back would be satisfying. What a special day it had been!

. . .

When the actual reunion day arrived, my father would pull in to the farm's gravel driveway ever so slowly. Cars painted in rich colors of that era would already be parked under the shade trees, their large headlights, visors, and heavy chrome gleaming in the sunlight.

But there was really one, and only one, car we were looking for: a large, elegant one in a rich dark color, either an Oldsmobile or a Cadillac. Not only would it be far more beautiful than any of the rest of our cars, it had come the furthest. It had made the fifteen hundred mile trip once again to this very farm, all the way from Montana. Aunt Mildred and Uncle Ted were here!

Why, in those years, Montana seemed as far away to us as another continent does today! Once again, Aunt Mildred and Uncle Ted had driven all that way to visit us. It was obvious that such a trip warranted nothing short of a grand gathering, a family reunion! Their presence was a great honor, and we were ready to properly welcome our special guests from the West.

You see, all of the Burows, starting in the late 1800's with my grandfather Emil and his brother (this very Ted who was actually my great uncle), had been born right in Jefferson County. And all of Emil's and Nelly's five children had stayed right in Jefferson County, except my father who had only gone as far away as Chicago for his accounting education, and then to Racine with his new bride after the Second World War.

Even though my uncles Leslie and Eldyn had gone to fight the War, they had come back to Jefferson, to marry and settle there. My Uncle Bun had never even left this family farm. When he married Virginia they had moved right in to help his parents. The brothers' only sister, my aunt Marie, was really just down the road a bit on a farm in Lake Mills with her husband Algene Jacobson and their family. Everyone in the family had seemed to find their place, working hard and building satisfying lives, content to live in or near Jefferson County's familiar surroundings.

. . .

Uncle Ted going West as a teen. He is on the right.

So although not one of us ever planned to live elsewhere, we were in awe of Uncle Ted's bold move to the West. He had left Wisconsin to build the telegraph lines as a teenager and after that work was finished, he had stayed to become a brakeman on the railroad. His train route ran through the most rugged mountains with the most treacherous conditions. Ted had married Mildred, a Montana gal, and they had settled in Three Forks, a small but strategic railroad town close to Yellowstone Park.

It was obvious to all of us that Ted was strong, intelligent, and fearless–our family's hero. Details from him were unnecessary, but they were not to be had anyway because our hero was a man of few words. Uncle Ted might matter-of-factly describe an episode he had encountered in the treacherous mountains, but he would never brag. That didn't matter to us because we knew the truth about him. Instead, Ted showed an interest in *our* Jefferson County lives! He would flash a handsome smile and give the men an encouraging pat on the back. We knew beyond a doubt that he cared about us. Why, hadn't he come over a thousand miles to see us?

. . .

In those reunion years, Uncle Ted was already approaching age sixty. I remember him looking like Yul Brynner. Baldness accentuated his striking face with high cheekbones and tightly drawn skin free of wrinkles. He still had perfect posture and a trim physique. Uncle Ted's clothes were impeccable: tailored suits of an expensive light wool fabric with stylish suspenders and vest over a white long-sleeved shirt. Frequently Ted would pull out a gold pocket watch to check the time, which we knew was a mark of a real railroad man.

We cousins remember Mildred resembling Aunt Bea from the *Andy Griffith* television show, with the same silver-gray hair pulled up in a loose bun. Her clothes were also impeccable with beautiful floral print silk dresses. And no matter how hot the Jefferson weather or the farm kitchen, she wore nylon stockings and jewelry and perfume. The main difference between Aunt Mildred and Aunt Bea, however, was that in some of those reunion years, Aunt Mildred's size was far greater than Aunt Bea's.

. . .

It may seem surprising, then, that having these two guests of honor in our midst actually presented a problem or two for us. For one, we simply could not curtail our curiosity about them. It was as if we were watching famous celebrities. Kindly as they were to us, it still seemed that these relatives were from another world! As we watched and listened, our curiosity then led to another problem. The more we scrutinized Uncle Ted and Aunt Mildred, the more we were faced with finding some flaws!

So when my parents and I finally arrived in that driveway, I would jump out of the car to look for Kenny, who was my age and my kindred spirit. We would find a safe place behind the farm house so that he could secretly describe the various idiosyncrasies he had noticed since Uncle Ted and Aunt Mildred had arrived. (How embarrassed I am today to think of our behavior and how sorrowful still that Kenny has been gone for almost fifty years and is not here to tell this story with me.)

The main foible with our hero seemed to be that although we never doubted Ted's mastery of Montana, it seemed that in other ways, Mildred was the master of Ted. It was Mildred who would commandingly drive most of the long trip to Wisconsin, roaring in to the farm driveway on arrival. It was Mildred who would order Ted, some times in a high-pitched tone, to fetch this or that item for her. And unfortunately, Kenny and I were not kind about Aunt Mildred's size.

But when Kenny came to describing how Aunt Mildred and Uncle Ted treated their dogs, he would barely be able to tell me his stories because he would be doubled over with laughter. In those days, on that farm, animals were treated as animals and not as if they were human. In comparison, Uncle Ted and Aunt Mildred seemed to have crossed that line. Each of their cocker spaniels, first Ring and later Bruce (named, I believe, for the famous Westminster cocker spaniel champion) were treated like kings. Two dogs could not have found a better life. Why else would a rail-road man travel thousands of miles by car to Jefferson, rather than by train, unless to chauffeur his dog? (Oh, how I was to smile many years later when my husband and I drove our very own cocker spaniel all the way from Wisconsin to Arizona when we moved there!)

One of Kenny's stories told about an afternoon when Mildred sent Ted into Jefferson to purchase the

*Uncle Ted and Aunt Mildred pose with their Cadillac
and cocker spaniel Bruce at the farm in 1963.
Our 1958 Chevrolet is in the background.*

highest quality meat for Bruce's supper, as the farm's beef had proven unsatisfactory upon inspection to her that day. But when Ted returned, that meat also failed to meet Mildred's standards. In a fury, Ted was dispatched back to town a second time so that Bruce could be fed properly!

Now, none of these episodes seriously detracted from our firm knowledge that Aunt Mildred and Uncle Ted were worthy of our greatest admiration and our appreciation. We would wait for a few years until they were coming again. We would gather once again, proud to have them in our midst. But we were left with the task of facing the fact that our relatives were indeed human. (And perhaps Aunt Mildred and Uncle Ted were faced with the very same task!)

.   .   .

Over the decades, the precious reunion days led to some of us making our own great trips to the West, to Three Forks. Although my parents never felt free from their work, nevertheless we were one family to make that trip. We took the train, as a drive to Montana at forty-five miles an hour on the back roads would never have worked! I was ten when we took the dome car through snow-covered mountains and narrow passes to arrive in Three Forks as if we were on a state visit.

Aunt Mildred, the proud Montana resident, was most excited to show us Yellowstone National Park. We were awestruck with Old Faithful and its lodge, the bears that walked right up to the cars, and the spectacular waterfalls. But my cautious parents found out all too well that the Yellowstone roads were not like Jefferson County's. They had hair-pin curves and edges with drop-offs to thousands of feet below. At high speeds that my parents could not begin to comprehend, Aunt Mildred would drive with one hand while petting Bruce with the other, pointing out the sights flying past us. Some of those sights were white painted crosses marking the deaths of fellow travelers. My mother, with her migraine headaches, was sure we were to be next.

.   .   .

Our grand family reunions of that era came to a close with the passing of Aunt Mildred and then Uncle Ted. In truth, the reunions had comprised just a few hours of our lives, but the memories of those days were never to end. We had welcomed our family heroes together. We had learned from each other and inspired each other. We had found that none of us were perfect, but we did not have to be. We belonged to each other. We were a family! The effort to be together had been well worth it!

So today if you travel past the spot where the Burow farm once stood and head down to Evergreen Cemetery, you will find two unassuming grave markers, one for Mildred and one for Ted Burow, that belie the special status we accorded them and that they surely deserved. As I write in many stories of my family, they have joined there in another reunion with so many of the other relatives from those memorable days, including my grandparents Emil and Nelly, Aunt Virginia and Uncle Bun, Uncle Leslie and Aunt Esther, cousin Kenny and cousin Lynn, and my own precious parents Ann and Wilmer. No, they are not on the farm, but they are gathered together at Evergreen, and I believe together in spirit, for a perfect and lasting reunion.

But what I like to do the most is to turn back the clocks in my mind to those hot reunion days and to let my memories float before my eyes. There we are, just pulling in to the driveway. The Cadillac is there!

And so, as always, I will keep my calendar open again this season, so that at a moment's notice, I can be with my family once more at another grand summer reunion.

17.

~ The Story That Came to Life ~

THERE was one number in our Racine telephone directory that was the most important to my parents. It was so important that they called it at least once a day and some times several times a day. It was telephone number 3-7731, the number for TIME. From an authoritative voice, they would hear: "Courtesy of your telephone company, THE TIME IS…"

My parents wanted to know the right time, not the time from the kitchen clock that could run fast or slow and might run down completely if not wound up. Not even the time from my father's gold Gruen wrist watch that had to be left regularly at the jeweler's for cleaning. And obviously not the time from the neighborhood clock tower above the Horlick's Malted Milk plant that chimed only on the hour.

My parents needed the right time, the exact time because then they knew just how many minutes my father had to make it to his next business appointment. Every single minute counted because, as he frequently stated to Mother and me, he was "pressed for time." And then he would be out the door...

.   .   .

You see, in those days my father was making up for lost time. The Depression and World War II had delayed his plans to become a certified public accountant and now that he finally was one, he worked night and day, often with my mother's help, to build up his business.

But that left little of his time for Mother and me. Mother's dinners might grow cold while he met with one more client. Her hopes of sitting together on our beautiful front porch at 1418 Carlisle Avenue never happened on a summer evening. And she wished, in vain, that he would find time to go with us to church on Sundays. Of course, we knew that he cared about us—well, we were quite certain that he did...

.   .   .

How we loved it, though, when he did have time to spend with us! I still smile remembering the few minutes here and there when he stopped to joke with my childhood playmates out on the lawn, even snapping a black and white photo of us lined up in front of our picket fence. I was thrilled when I saw him arrive (usually at the last minute) to sit with Mother for my Lincoln School programs, never failing to take time afterward to compliment me. I loved our occasional evening walks to Marigold Dairy for a chocolate malt. And then there were the beautiful greeting cards picked-out at Haas Drug Store for Mother, addressed in his fine penmanship, that she propped-up for days on the kitchen ledge.

.   .   .

There was one way, however, one certain way, to spend time with my father. It was the drive out to Jefferson. My father had never forgotten his boyhood home, although he had left it years before. There were "the relatives" to visit and many old friends, including my mother's, because she had spent years in Jefferson County herself as a teacher before marrying my father. Frankly, though, I suspect that we went to Jefferson just as much, if not more, for my father to meet with his clients.

One would never have guessed by watching our green 1952 Pontiac traveling toward Jefferson, however, that right before leaving, my hurried parents had telephoned for the TIME. Because no matter how pressed for time my father said he was, he rarely increased his driving speed to more than forty-five miles an hour. Nothing could make him go faster, not even a long line of honking cars behind us.

So at times, those sixty-five mile trips could seem to take us forever. But most of the time, they were not long enough. Because we were together.

.   .   .

It was on those trips that I loved to ask my father to tell me his stories about growing up in Jefferson even though every one was familiar to me. I had asked to hear them time and again. His stories never failed to fascinate me. I would try to imagine him, the man seated ahead of me in a tailor-made suit, as a boy in a completely different world. That world seemed so unlike the one I knew, that I felt as if I were watching a movie.

I would secretly marvel when he described walking to school four miles on muddy country roads or studying by kerosene lamp in the farm kitchen. I would be amazed to picture him with a horse and buggy, covered with the family's heavy robe on freezing winter nights. And it seemed as if I were watching a musical when I pictured the farm neighbors gathered after a barn-raising for music and dancing.

I can hear that child's voice now from the back seat saying, "Dad, tell me the one about…"

.　　.　　.

My father's most melancholic story was about his younger brother Claire's fall from the barn's hayloft to the cement floor below, soon resulting in a brain tumor. About how their father took his seriously ill son by train to far-off Milwaukee desperately seeking treatment, only to eventually drive a horse and wagon during a violent rain storm, with my young father seated beside him, to bury the child at Evergreen Cemetery.

There was the dramatic story of my father's "Runaway" when he was about eight and in charge of a team of horses pulling a huge wagonload of household goods as the family moved to yet another rental farm on March 1st, the day farm leases were up. The startled horses leaped out of his control after hearing a train whistle, careening over the countryside for miles, only stopping when they were exhausted rather than responding to the frantic efforts of the panic-stricken boy. (Mother and I believed that this very episode may have explained my father's slow driving!)

There was the heroic one about my grandfather Emil single-handedly winning a tug of war. When a belligerent farm neighbor challenged him to a tug of war against the man's strongest teen-age son, my grandfather accepted the challenge on one condition, that all five of the man's sons pull simultaneously together against him on the other end. Cannily selecting the right place in the farm yard to dig his heel firmly into the ground, my grandfather gave a powerful sudden jerk that instantly felled them all.

And there was the Depression story describing the shock one early morning as news spread like wild fire across the county that the Jefferson banks were closed.

．　．　．

There were the hilarious stories about my father in his young days, including his travels with the Jefferson city band in borrowed hearses and ambulances to perform their concert forty miles away. There were stories of his teen-age pranks, like hoisting a hay wagon to the top of the country school roof one night, creating the exact astonishment hoped for in the morning.

There was the amusing story about my father at his country school's evening Christmas program when Santa Claus entered to surprise the children. My father was stunned to notice that the visitor was wearing a neck scarf that did not belong to him! In indignation, he called out to accuse Santa Claus of wearing Emil Burow's clothing!

．　．　．

And then there was the most amazing story of all, about Morris C. Kiltz, his 1920's high school classmate. My father would describe this unusual person, who was an enigma to Jefferson residents. Morris C. Kiltz, who always stated his complete name, frightened many people with his shaggy dark-haired, unkempt appearance and his severe stutter. He seemed to roam the city from the mysterious, dilapidated home he lived in down by the river. (In an attempt to explain this strange local character, it was rumored that Morey had been struck in the head years before.)

But Morris C. Kiltz was strange in another way, in an astounding way. He possessed the most incredible memory anyone in Jefferson had ever witnessed. For instance, my father would describe how Morris could recall the scores of any national baseball game and the statistics of any player. No one could stump him and no one had ever seen anything like it!

For his amazing memory, Morey earned the astonished admiration of everyone in Jefferson and the amused acceptance of the high school chums who nevertheless found ways to trick him. Morris would run at top speed around an entire down town block in Jefferson, believing that the local boys were accurately timing him.

. . .

So when we three arrived in Jefferson, after hearing my favorite stories, I would look up and down the streets and the roads and see it all in a different light. I could look right at the two stately Jefferson banks, but also see them as they once were, closed to their frightened depositors. I could watch the band playing right on the city square and imagine the members piling into an ambulance or two for the ride to another performance. I could pass a long-abandoned one-room country school and picture a hay wagon on its roof. And I loved to spot my young father and his high school chums gathered on the street corners with the local character Morris C. Kiltz.

It was as if I were still watching a movie.

.　　.　　.

There was an important difference, however, about the Morris C. Kiltz story compared to all the others. While the subjects of the others existed mainly in the past, Morris C. Kiltz was actually still alive. In fact, every year a beautiful religious Christmas card arrived from Chicago, with his full name scrawled in large handwriting.

The card would prompt my father to tell his familiar stories once again and to marvel that his classmate was surviving in such a large city. From the network of high school friends, my father knew that Morris worked for the railroad. It was said in Jefferson that Morris C. Kiltz could remember the exact location of

> * MAY HE *
> GRANT YOU BLESSINGS
> * AT CHRISTMAS *
> TO BRIGHTEN THE
> WHOLE YEAR THROUGH

Mr. and Mrs.
Wilmer E. Burow and Carol
From Morris & Kitty

The annual Christmas card from Morris

every railroad car in the Chicago system and that he could recall a complete timetable without looking at a piece of paper.

My parents would be certain to send their Christmas greetings, sincerely wishing Morey the best. But it

12-18-77

Dear Morris:

I asked one of the supervisors at Western Printing Company to see if he could get some labels. If he finds some, I will send them to you.

Merry Christmas, Morris.

Your long-time friend,

W. E. Burow

My father's annual greeting to Morris

was not in their plans to see him. For one thing, my father was too pressed for time to even think about such things.

.   .   .

Then one Saturday summer evening when I was of grade school age, as Mother and I stood talking together on our front lawn while she finished her gardening, a taxi cab pulled up to the curb right in front of our house. As we stopped to watch this unusual sight, out stepped a gray-haired stranger whose stooped, slovenly appearance was enough to frighten my mother, kind and caring though she was.

Haltingly introducing himself to Mother and me, the man announced his full name. The passenger was none other than Morris C. Kiltz, astonishingly come to life from the stories I had heard. Fortunately my father was at home to hear from Morris C. Kiltz that he had come to personally invite my parents to his church's forthcoming anniversary celebration. Following those words, our visitor was ready to depart on the next train back to Chicago.

Now each of my parents faced a dilemma. My kind mother was a person of genuine faith and a dedicated church member, so surely it seemed that she would accept. But try as she might, her fears of this alarming character and what she might encounter in his Chicago neighborhood clearly prevented her from going. My father was obviously too pressed for time and, frankly, uninterested in a church's anniversary celebration.

But on the appointed date, and surely after calling for the TIME to be ready at the very last minute, my father and my father alone, in tailored suit and tie, was on the train to Chicago to attend the church celebration. While Mother and I worried about him that evening, he arrived home safely after midnight. I seem to recall the words "skid row" in his description of where he had been, including a stifling apartment near the railroad yard.

.   .   .

Looking back, I might have expected my father to turn his trip to Chicago into another amusing story, perhaps even told to his advantage at the expense of another. But it never became one. Instead, I believe that he simply viewed it as a most natural thing to do—to honor his boyhood friend from Jefferson, Morris C. Kiltz.

.   .   .

In time, both friends were to return to their boyhood home of Jefferson County. Morris C. Kiltz was buried in 1993 in the city of Jefferson's Union Cemetery. My father came to his resting place on June 14, 1995, in Fort Atkinson's Evergreen Cemetery.

18.

~ A Hilltop Farm ~

I REMEMBER my father finding the long winding driveway almost hidden from view by the high summer corn, and taking it up up up ever so carefully to the top of the ridge. I remember the sound of gravel crunching under our car tires as we slowly climbed to finally see a pleasant cream-colored frame house and bright red barn at the top. And then to also see clothes drying on the line, a summer garden with rows of dark purple gladiolas, pink phlox, and bright zinnias, a slightly slanted wooden garage and a slatted corn crib nearby, and a tractor or two dotting the yard's perimeter.

I remember the silence of the car motor stopping and then my mother's happiness in seeing her sister come out to greet us from the farm house, quickly drying her hands on her apron as she came toward us. Joy filled the sunny air.

I remember bringing our suitcases into the silent, dark house with the shades down against the heat, to the bedroom off of the dining room, with its linoleum floor, with its window open and the curtains flapping in the breeze. I remember the dresser with the wavy mirror and crocheted cloth on its top, the bed, with its chenille spread and squeaky metal springs. And there was the roll-away stored for me in the corner.

Next, I see my father carrying in his briefcase and his bulky black Burroughs adding machine to the dining room table, my aunt Ingeborg eagerly pulling back the lacy tablecloth so that he could spread out his accountant's working papers. I see her hovering over him to learn that he had everything he needed. An afternoon of accounting work was what suited him.

.   .   .

And then, as always, I would go out on the front porch or the front lawn to spread my blanket. I would unpack my books and colors and puzzles and dolls and arrange them for my afternoon. The sweeping view of the green valley below opened in front of me like the center pages of a fabulous picture book ready for a ten-year-old to gaze upon.

I remember waiting for Uncle Ben to come in

from the fields for supper, noticing his wide smile and big gnarled hands. And supper! With Mother and Aunt "Ing" working pleasantly together most of the afternoon in the kitchen, they set the table with fluffy white mashed potatoes, a tender pot roast, cucumbers with cream and dill, thick red tomato slices, and perhaps corn on the cob. (All delicious but the milk, never to my liking, because of its thick texture and heavy cream taste far different from that of the city's!)

.   .   .

I remember the porch at sunset. After the supper dishes were done, Mother, Aunt Ing, my father and I would go out to the rocking chairs and watch the orange ball slowly sinking behind the dimming valley. When Uncle Ben came in after milking, we would all sit together, eating creamy mounds of vanilla ice cream in sweet cantaloupe shells, bidding goodnight to a perfect summer day far away from the world's cares.

.   .   .

On a beautiful summer late afternoon a few years ago, I searched for a hidden driveway. When at last I felt certain that I had found it, I took it slowly up up up. With bated breath I found myself hoping to find the scene at the top exactly as I remembered it. Of course that was not meant to be. The owner, gracious to a stranger, instead allowed me the time to take in the modern changes to the house and the barn.

Then I turned, with my heart pounding, to find the spot where I had once spread my blanket and to imagine the front porch where we five had so often sat. *Had I somehow let myself hope that I would find the others there?* A wave of longing nearly overcame me.

As I stood alone on the hilltop, the orange sun began to sink over the dimming valley and the magnificent scene opened to me. How my heart leaped! The scene was exactly as I remembered. The hilltop farm was still ours.

19.

~ The Christmas Cactus ~

ON CHRISTMAS morning, our drive on country roads from Racine to my mother's home village of Rio in Wisconsin's Columbia County seemed to take forever! Oh, it was fun for me to sit in the back seat of our two-tone green Pontiac with my favorite dolls, wearing my new Christmas dress and black patent "Mary Janes." It was fun to spot the occasional strings of Burma Shave signs with their clever sayings along the road sides. But our trip always took far too long for a child waiting to celebrate Christmas day with her special aunts and uncles, and in the most special home of all.

Only after what seemed an eternity, would the steeple of Rio Redeemer Lutheran Church come in to view. It was finally then that I knew our destination was almost reached, the pretty white gingerbread house just down the street at 504 Lincoln Avenue, the home where Mother had grown up and where my grandmother and my uncle Andrew and aunt Elva lived now.

And then suddenly, the long drive soon forgotten, we would be at the front door, with Mother's dignified brother and his beautiful wife welcoming us. Her sister Ingeborg and husband Ben, my aunt and uncle, would already have arrived from their farm in Jefferson County. (On *any* occasion, we three were usually the last guests to arrive because my father was a notoriously slow driver. And perhaps as a conscientious certified public accountant focused on year-end tax planning for his clients, he was less than enthusiastic about the hours ahead that were sure to be filled with Norwegian lore!)

.　.　.

We would take off our coats and both of my aunts would turn me around to exclaim over my Christmas dress. My aged grandmother would be roused from a rest to join us. Then we would all visit in the charming living room with its beautiful Christmas tree while I surveyed the bookcases and the Norwegian mementos in their familiar places. Soon we would be called for Aunt Elva's delicious Christmas dinner in the dining

The house at 504 Lincoln Avenue in the early 1900's when my widowed grandmother bought it. She is standing with her children— my mother Ann next to her, Andrew, and Ingeborg.

room. Its table would be set with her beautiful china and we, too, would take our familiar places once again. Of course Uncle Andrew would begin with a prayer, usually recited in Norwegian. Reminiscing would follow about growing up in Rio and then our host and hostess would proudly deliver the current village news.

Andrew, Rio's respected attorney, was also a master historian, not only of Rio and of Wisconsin, but of the world! Even as a child, I realized the depth of his knowledge and was fascinated with how he brought the past to life and related it to current circumstances.

Uncle Ben would be asked about the fall harvest and milk prices. My father, however, would become visibly more enthusiastic if somehow the dinner conversation turned to taxes, his favorite topic! Then everyone would linger after dessert while Andrew translated letters from the Norwegian relatives he and Elva had met when they spent an entire summer in Europe. The clock on the elegant buffet would chime the time away.

Nevertheless, as much as I loved the Christmas dinner and the grown-ups' table conversations, after a time I would secretly wait for it to end. I knew what I wanted to do next. At long last, my mother and aunts would disappear into the kitchen to "do the dishes," never stopping their visiting for a minute. My grandmother would rest, and the men would return to the living room, supposedly to continue their dinner conversation, but in actuality, to doze.

It was then, that with my aunt Elva's permission, I would explore the old house.

· · ·

504 Lincoln Avenue was completely fascinating. I could sense the Fadness family history in its air! I knew its story well: how my brave grandmother had moved her little family from a farm into Rio, to this very house, when she became a young widow in the early 1900's. I could almost feel the love the three children

had for their mother, for her kindness to them and for her strength and courage. Why, my grandmother had cleaned the entire Rio high school herself each summer to make "ends meet." And she had greatly encouraged her children, even to attend far-off colleges in 1920! I loved to imagine my mother as a girl walking through these very rooms, looking like the sepia photos I had seen of her in lacy white dresses with her long braided hair tied in ribbons.

And then I loved seeing all of the beautiful antiques and Norwegian pieces in their familiar places. Aunt Elva would repaint the gleaming white woodwork or replace wallpapers and drapes occasionally, but overall, the house kept its same stately look.

But most intriguing of all were the mysteries I found at 504 Lincoln Avenue. For one thing, the Rio house contained not one, but two staircases. And they were not open staircases, but *hidden* staircases!

On top of that, I found a mysterious object in every room.

.   .   .

I would always set out to explore the house in exactly the same order. Beginning in the master bedroom on the first floor, I would open a white door that a stranger might think was simply a closet door. But no! This very door opened to a hidden staircase! I would climb

*One of my mother's countless visits to her mother at the
Rio house—this scene in the 1930's*

the winding, steep, narrow steps, covered with the colorful Norwegian carpet runner my grandmother had crocheted. Cold air would hit my face as I climbed.

At the top, I would arrive in the boyhood bedroom of Peter and John, the sons of my aunt and uncle, who were now away in the armed services. Two twin maple beds were perfectly made with white chenille spreads. Fading high school pennants hung on the sloping walls that were papered in a small gray print. The polished wooden floor gleamed. But it was the huge trunk, covered with scrolls of Norwegian rosemaling, that commanded my attention. It was mysterious! I would stand in front of it, imagining its voyage over the ocean long years before. I would picture my grandmother at seventeen, watching over her trunk that contained her precious possessions headed for America.

Next, I would walk along a narrow open corridor with a spindled railing on my left, looking over it to the home's second staircase. At the passage's end, I would stand at the doorway of another bedroom, knowing that I would see an antique bed so high off of the floor that I wondered how anyone could climb on to it. Its carved wooden headboard reached almost to the ceiling. However, it was the large portrait on the far wall that held this room's mystery. To think that the stranger was Mother's father, my grandfather, who had died of appendicitis when she was three. Only this

The mysterious looking portrait of my grandfather,
Lewis Fadness, that hung in an upstairs bedroom

portrait, with his piercing eyes looking directly at me, seemed to prove that he had once existed.

Continuing along the corridor, and hurrying past Uncle Andrew's mounted deer head that seemed way too close to me for comfort, I would carefully open a door that was always tightly shut. It was the door to the mysterious "storeroom." Here, possessions were piled helter-skelter to the ceiling. There were pieces of antique furniture, lamps and lamp shades, suitcases, picnic baskets, books and stacks of magazines. A drawn yellowed window shade allowed just enough light to show dust particles filtering through the cold musty air. But what was most amazing, was that these possessions were my mother's! During the many years she had been a teacher until she married my father "late in life," she had never had a home of her own. Instead, the Rio house had held her possessions until the day she could come to claim them, a day that Mother knew was now long overdue. (Perhaps right at this very minute, Mother was downstairs assuring Aunt Elva that this was surely going to be the spring when she would come for them!)

. . .

Reluctantly, I would slowly descend the second hidden staircase, not wanting my exploring to end. As I opened the door at the bottom to the parlor, I would imagine the surprise I might cause to unsuspecting guests if they were seated there when I emerged! But at Christmas, I had the pretty room to myself, with its upright piano, my grandmother's wooden rocking chairs, an ornate table topped with Norwegian keep-sakes and a fascinating antique postcard stereoscope, all facing out to Lincoln Avenue.

Finally, my gaze would go to a wooden stand that displayed this room's mysterious object. It was the "Christmas Cactus," a large, green plant with strange leaves that looked like drooping tentacles. I knew that it was revered by my mother, my aunts and my uncle because it had been started so long ago by my grand-mother. To me, however, it bore no resemblance to the prickly cactuses I had seen in pictures and certainly not to Christmas! And it certainly did not look beau-tiful! However, year after year, the mysterious cactus kept its honored place.

My exploration over once again, I would rejoin the grown-ups seated together in the living room, now talking over world events and the events of this little family and of Rio.

.   .   .

When the sad day arrived when my grandmother passed away at age ninety-two, Andrew and Elva became the sole owners of 504 Lincoln Avenue. My grandmother's possessions from the precious old house were divided among the three siblings. Mother received her rocking chairs, crocheted tablecloths and pillow cases, paintings, glassware, china, books, and of course her own treasures from the storeroom. And she also received the mysterious Christmas Cactus.

Being an artist, Mother had ingeniously decorated our own home in Racine. Now she could add the keepsakes from 504 Lincoln Avenue to her collections at 1418 Carlisle Avenue. She placed the Christmas Cactus on a stand in our living room, where it stayed under her care, for the next thirty years. And for thirty years, I continued to view the strange drooping green plant, with its inappropriate Christmas Cactus name, as simply a mysterious object.

Ever so slowly, however, I began to respect its increasing importance as a part of Fadness family history.

. . .

And then, we were without Mother. Oh, how we missed her! Married and living one hour away from my father who steadfastly remained on Carlisle Avenue, I regularly visited him. I would find myself exploring the quiet old house, room by room, just as I had 504 Lincoln Avenue. Occasionally, I offered to add a few new decorating touches to Mother's beautiful arrangements, but I soon learned not to. My father would firmly say, "Carol, we need to keep it the way Ann had it." So for ten years, we kept everything the way Ann had it. And that included keeping the Christmas Cactus alive, its mysterious green, drooping appearance never changing.

.   .   .

And then it was my dear father who passed away. How I missed him, as well as Mother, even though I had a wonderful husband and daughter. The time had come to take the precious possessions from Carlisle Avenue to my own home, to be incorporated just as Mother had once done with her Lincoln Avenue keepsakes.

Now, my home had the Carlisle baby grand piano, its grandfather clock, its glassware and books, a few furniture pieces kept from that home's original owner and Mother's carefully chosen used "treasures" from Racine's Earl the Trader. And it had my artist mother's own beautiful paintings.

It also had a Norwegian trunk, carved wooden rocking chairs, and crocheted linens from Lincoln Avenue. And it had the Christmas Cactus. The old plant took its place in my living room, on the same little stand Mother had selected for it. Despite its appearance that had never been to my liking, I was now ready to give it its well-deserved place of prominence. After all, it had been a part of our family for at least fifty years and perhaps, just perhaps, far longer than that.

.   .   .

As the first Christmas approached without my parents, I found myself profoundly missing them. On

The miraculous Christmas Cactus

some moments, I dreaded the approaching holiday. Until one afternoon.

As I happened to walk through my living room, I stopped short. *Had I seen something out of the corner of my eye? A speck of pink color?* I held my breath, and hesitatingly retraced my steps to the Christmas Cactus. There it was, one pink blossom among the green drooping leaves, perhaps the first one in fifty years. I instantly felt my mother's presence.

That Christmas season, the mysterious old plant was ablaze in pink color, becoming the most beautiful plant in the world as it delivered a miraculous message from all of those dear people from the past who had cared for it. My loved ones were with me on Christmas.

. . .

Today, that first magical pink blossom is carefully preserved among my family treasures. And the beautiful old Christmas Cactus itself continues to hold a prominent place in my home. Each Christmas, I wait with baited breath until it miraculously blooms once again. Some day, I hope that it will provide the same miracle for our precious daughter in her home.

Section III
~ HOME AGAIN...FOREVER ~

Love never dies as long as there is someone who remembers.

~Leo Buscaglia

20.

~ Home for Christmas ~

FINALLY, it was Christmas vacation! Classes were over, lockers were slammed shut, and boisterous good-byes had faded into silence. At last, Karen and I were driving out of our high school parking lot in her family's stylish white Dodge Coronet.

As excited as we were to be high school juniors in that year of 1964, it had been a hectic semester, studying hard for the honor roll, working on Homecoming and the school newspaper, and starting to plan for college. We were ready for vacation! And we knew exactly how we would spend it. After all, Karen and I had grown up in our hometown, and we had been friends since grade school.

We would Christmas shop downtown, in the

familiar stores we knew so well: Zahn's, our grand department store for a complete variety of presents, and Eitel's and Feiges Brothers for sweater sets and camel coats. Joseph Lawrence would provide us with the best ties and shirts for our fathers or Mohr-Jones Hardware for any tool they might want. Perhaps across town we would shop at The Loom of Denmark for the most modern Scandinavian household items.

At night we would join the long line of cars that wound its way slowly past the Wheary family's astonishing display of white lights covering their enormous pine trees. We would stop in at classmates' homes who hosted evening "coffee houses" in their basements, where high school friends sang and played guitars, faithfully copying Pete Seeger, The Kingston Trio, and Peter, Paul and Mary. In between, we would stop in at Kewpee's for hamburgers and malts, or hot fudge sundaes at Big Boy.

Of course we would spend time at each other's houses. And needless to say, wherever we were, we would be wondering if and when a Christmas romance might come our way.

Indeed, our vacation did unfold as we expected— until late one afternoon.

.   .   .

In my upstairs bedroom on that afternoon, Karen

and I leisurely watched the Carlisle Avenue street lights beginning to glow, highlighting lacy patterns of the gently falling snow. Colored Christmas tree lights began to shine from the picture windows up and down the boulevard.

But amidst this tranquil setting, our conversation suddenly took an unexpected turn. Karen and I faced facts that we had never quite noticed before. Why, life in our hometown was actually stifling us! It was entirely *too* familiar, *too* predictable. We needed broader experiences than our hometown could possibly offer us!

Likewise, a solution came to us just as suddenly. We would go to New York City that summer.

Of course neither of us had been to New York, nor did we know anyone else who had ever been there. In our middle class way of life, few families we knew in Racine even went regularly to Chicago, just one hundred miles down the shore of Lake Michigan. My own parents had each been to Washington, D.C. in their single days, but never New York. Such a trip would be a complete impossibility as they worked constantly to build up my father's accounting business.

Karen's parents had met in Europe during the War, and although they often went to Chicago, leaving the great Midwest with their three children had never been a consideration.

Nevertheless, Karen and I felt certain that our parents would understand our situation. Obtaining their approval even seemed quite unnecessary.

Carlisle Avenue may have looked like a familiar tranquil winter setting that afternoon, but two girls suddenly saw it in a different light. They were changed forever.

.   .   .

After a thorough study, we settled on the Greyhound for our means of transportation. For lodging, we were impressed to learn that as members of Racine's YWCA, we were part of a vast network, including the Laura Spellman Y at 840 8th Avenue, conveniently located right near 5th Avenue. Its brochure featured a modern bright orange lobby.

Our itinerary was simple. We would see everything we could possibly see, until the money we were saving ran out.

.   .   .

Suddenly it was the long-awaited day of our June departure. The next morning, we were in New York City.

Now two girls were to learn what "marketing" means. The Laura Spellman's attractive lobby of the brochure had faded into decay. Our stifling seventh floor room was so close to the clanging elevator that we may as well have been in it. And the ancient porcelain knobs on the bathroom sink occasionally fell off. In a few brief minutes, we had become much wiser to the world.

Realizing, however, that we would need to stay at the Laura Spellman, our sight-seeing could begin in earnest. First, to the top of the highest building in the world, the Empire State. Then, day by day, to Rockefeller Center, NBC studios, Central Park, St. Patrick's Cathedral, and to Dr. Norman Vincent Peale at the Marble Collegiate Church. We were in the audience of *The Price is Right* and on the tour boat around Manhattan. Spending hours at the staid Metropolitan Museum and the modern Guggenheim, we then cautiously viewed "hippies" in Greenwich Village. When the expense of Broadway was too great, we simply substituted Radio City's *Rockettes*. We were entirely satisfied.

Each evening we ate at the Horn & Hardart automat or at Tad's Steak House, both selected for economic reasons. The automat was amazingly modern with selected sandwiches dropping out of machines at a low cost. Tad's gave us the appearance of finer dining even though we knew that the prices and the quality were near rock bottom. Then we would return to the Laura Spellman before dark and take the long, slow, jangling ride up the elevator to our stifling room. Another adventurous day had been accomplished!

.   .   .

Now we had another inspiration! Since we were already on the East Coast, perhaps we should hop down to Washington, D.C. to see our country's national monuments. Already familiar with the Greyhound, we could certainly rely on it for our transportation. However, the ride was longer than we thought and the blast of stifling summer air that met us as we got off the bus was nothing like the heartland's.

We had much to accomplish in fewer hours than we had thought, and all on foot because of our dwindling budget. The Capitol was massive, the Lincoln Monument stirring, the Washington stately. However, the distance between them was on a far larger scale than we had imagined from the postcards and guidebooks we had consulted. As the temperature increased, so did the blisters on our feet.

Returning to the Laura Spellman that night, we were entirely pleased with our unexpected side trip to the nation's capital, dismissing any disappointment that our ambitious itinerary had been necessarily curtailed.

.   .   .

Karen...

...and Carol sightseeing in New York City

For two rather sheltered girls, it was surprising that Karen and I seldom thought about home. We had called our parents on arrival, but in those days, long distance calls were a rarity. Now early one morning, our room's black rotary-dial telephone rang loudly. When I answered it, my mother's voice was amazingly clear. I soon learned why. My parents were in the Laura Spellman lobby.

Karen and I were in shock! But I was also mortified. From my point of view, I was in imminent danger of losing my adventure. In the lobby, I spoke to them guardedly with Karen acting as a kind mediator. We learned that they had come by train in the night and thank goodness, they already had a hotel. That morning was the only time we spent together in New York City.

Coincidentally, Karen and I were beginning to think of home. Our funds were getting low, and it was time to make plans to return. I arrived in Racine to an empty house. My parents were staying on in New York!

.   .   .

Now almost fifty years have passed since that New York City trip. During those decades, there have been many trips for Karen, as well as for me, with our husbands and children, even to far more distant places than New York.

And there have also been trips to Racine, the

hometown we found so stifling in our teens. In time, our youthful desire to leave our hometown was replaced for Karen and for me with appreciation for the privilege of returning to this familiar place of our roots and to the people we loved.

It was on Christmas, especially, that we longed to be there. And indeed, for thirty more years I had the privilege of returning to 1418 Carlisle Avenue on Christmas, to the very home where we first thought up our New York City trip. And for almost fifty years, Karen could return to her home where we would sit together in the living room we had known since childhood.

As the years increased, so did our reminiscing. Year after year our Christmas visits with our precious parents turned to the fond memories we shared, and of course to the grand New York City trip. We marveled at the two teenage girls who dared to follow their astonishing dream that began so surprisingly on a Christmas vacation long ago. We recognized the love of parents that made them travel so far to learn in a few minutes that their daughter was safe. And we all forgave that daughter for her stand of independence.

. . .

And so this Christmas, once again, Karen and I hope to return with our families to our hometown.

A light snow may be falling as we take the bittersweet drive down Carlisle Avenue past "my" house, and then past Karen's. If only we could go inside!

But Christmas tree lights will be starting to shine from the picture windows. The Carlisle street lights will be shimmering down the center of the boulevard like a strand of pearls. For just a few magical moments, it seems as if time has stood still.

We are home for Christmas.

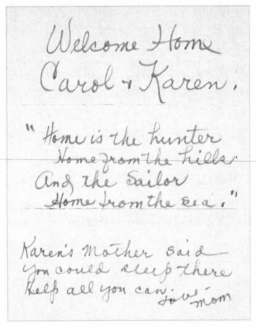

My mother's note welcoming us home, written with her supposition that Karen and I might return before my parents.

21.

~ Double Vision ~

I FIRST encountered double vision when I was much younger (in my forty's) and when I did not yet suffer from the condition myself. The surprising discovery of this vision problem in others first occurred at a family reunion, leaving me dumb-founded and, actually, quite amused. Little did I realize that I would contract the very same condition within a decade.

I had decided to attend the family reunion which was on my mother's side. Upon first reading the invitation, I learned that the Fadnesses would gather at Keyeser, a sleepy Wisconsin crossroads in Columbia County, at the country church located on one of four corners. My mother had loved her home area and I was especially nostalgic because she had recently passed away. I had been to this church a few times in my childhood, including my grandmother's funeral. I could still remember my mother's sadness and her warm, soft hand over mine on that day.

My only reservation about the reunion was that I would know very few of my relatives. My mother had remained extremely close to her brother Andrew and sister Ingeborg and their families all of her life, but not to a larger extended Fadness clan, mainly because our own family lived in Racine and the distance was too great to make regular visits to other relatives. I had listened to Mother's fond stories about the relatives over the years, but in reality, only my first cousin John and his wife Lois would be at the reunion to greet me. Nevertheless, I sent in my reply and set out for this green, rolling Wisconsin countryside, the county my mother had loved, for what I hoped would be a heart-warming summer weekend.

. . .

When I arrived, the church basement was impressively set-up with blackboards, tracing intricate Fadness family trees. There were Fadnesses poring over old black and white and sepia photos, some using magnifying glasses to better identify our ancestors. The cemetery, adjacent to the church, was marked with flags designating the graves of our most significant forbearers, starting with Knut, the first Fadness to arrive from Norway. (I recalled that his lichen-covered tall grave stone bore the barely visible carving: 1.) And of course the church's Ladies' Aid Society had prepared a delicious lunch, with plenty of the home-made rolls, ham, potato salads, and chocolate desserts I loved.

But it was the bus tour that was to acquaint me with double vision. A yellow school bus waited to transport Fadnesses every half hour on a route of significant nearby sites. A numbered guide sheet showing the various stops we would make was distributed to everyone entering the bus.

My astonishment began immediately, however, with location number one, the blacksmith shop. When we arrived at this location, I was unable to see a blacksmith shop. In fact, I saw nothing but an empty field of waving grasses. But not so with my relatives! They exclaimed about the building, the owner, and the horses. But I still saw nothing.

Nearly every stop presented a spot that looked vacant to me, but not to my fellow relatives. They obviously had contracted double vision. When I returned home, I regaled my friends with stories about the tour of empty fields.

. . .

However, strange things happen! Within the decade,

I found myself acquiring the very same double vision condition exhibited by my relatives. I do not know precisely when I first noticed it. Perhaps it came on gradually. I remember that when I drove down Carlisle Avenue after both of my parents had passed away and 1418 Carlisle was no longer our home after owning it for forty-five years, the condition definitely progressed.

Instead of seeing new residents along the boulevard who were strangers to me, and homes that had changed since my childhood, I very clearly saw my old neighbors along the Avenue. Why, most certainly there was our next door neighbor, our friend Joe Arnone, walking home after work from Belle City! There was Emelia sitting on the porch, waiting supper for him.

And there was Gary Larsen, just home from high school, walking his black Labrador, Jet, perhaps over to our house to share one of his exciting tales of the day. "Otts" Olson, my friend Jackie's father, was also just arriving home from work, getting out of his little Nash Rambler. Soon he would be heading for Johnson's for a quick round of golf before dark. Or perhaps he would be going to relieve Jackie's mother Pauline at their Marigold Dairy on the end of Carlisle, ready to make us his delicious malts.

My favorite teachers at Lincoln School were surely walking out to their cars in their stylish suits and high heels at the end of the day! Wasn't that Mrs. Miller getting into her yellow 1957 T-Bird right now? And our beloved principal Mr. Temme, getting into his Buick on Hamilton Street? And at Haas Drug Store, both Mr. and Mrs. Haas were conscientiously filling prescriptions while waiting on their customers at the soda fountain. In fact, the big clock tower on the pristine grounds of the Horlick Malted Milk plant was chiming the hour right now!

And traveling down State Street, Orla's Barber Shop pole was surely turning! Wasn't he standing near his geranium-filled window, wearing his immaculate white coat? And surely I could detect the aroma in the air of Lincoln Bakery's ginger bars! Next door, people were entering the confectionary store for a newspaper and candy from the glass cabinets.

.　　.　　.

So, I have come to accept the fact that I, too, have acquired double vision. Perhaps I am older and wiser. Perhaps I am foolish. But with much keener insight since the Fadness reunion, I now quite firmly believe that double vision actually increases in direct proportion to the inevitable losses we accumulate over the years of the dear people and places we have loved.

The more I miss the grand drive down Carlisle Avenue from my childhood with its huge canopy of trees overhead and its milk-glass street lights, the

My dear parents and I in our backyard
of 1418 Carlisle Avenue during the 1960's

clearer its former appearance becomes. The more
I miss its old residents, I am certain to find them.

But for whom I am truly looking is my mother, who
made me feel as loved as any child could be. And I am
looking down the Avenue for my father, who remained
a solid source of strength as long as he was able. For
just a second, I see her, coming to our big oval front

door to lovingly greet me once again. And certainly that must be my father, in suit and tie, just returning home and getting out of his car on the boulevard.

The hope and the pleasure I receive from my vision condition is well worth it. I will not fight against it or look for a recovery.

~ Acknowledgements ~

ON THE NIGHT I sat down to write the story of our next door neighbors, Philip and Jeanette Weiler, it was simply for love remembered, a recollection for myself. I had no thought in mind that it might some day be part of a book. Now, looking back on almost ten years since that night, I can see the beautiful pattern of amazing people from the past and from the present who have brought that story and its companions into this volume.

Editor Christine Spangler immediately welcomed my stories into the *Daily Jefferson County Union* newspaper. Elizabeth Young, former feature editor of Racine's *Journal Times* newspaper, likewise found the early stories appealing and Ann Walter, as current editor, has continued to welcome them. Craig Spychalla of the *Portage Daily Register* has featured annual Christmas stories. Due to these talented people and their publications, over time readers became acquainted with my life at 1418 Carlisle Avenue and I gained courage to continue writing.

And then the writer Genevieve Sesto emailed me with a positive message after *The 1400 Block* appeared in Racine's newspaper. Unacquainted, we met and immediately found that we shared many of the same memories from the old neighborhood and many fond similarities regarding our parents. It soon became evident that if a book came to be, she would be my perfect editor. Genevieve has been a magnificent one, guiding and encouraging and improving all that appears in this book. In fact, there would not be a book without Genevieve, now my dear friend.

Next, Genevieve and I turned to Lucia Lozano for her creative book designing. Upon our very first meeting, we knew that she appreciated the purpose of the stories and would capture them in a beautiful fashion.

However, I simply could not think of a title. Interested people would ask me what it might be, only to look crestfallen when I stated my latest attempt. It was my friend Toni Crist Savaglio who suddenly offered *My Heart Leads Me Home*. I consider it perfect!

.   .   .

But how could I not acknowledge my precious parents, Ann Fadness Burow and Wilmer Elroy Burow? How I value the love and respect and guidance they gave me! It seems impossible that they have been gone since the 1990's. How I miss them! How I want to remember our life together! They are the star characters of this book. If they could read these little stories today, I hope they would be touched by their daughter's memories.

My pleasant memories are also filled with so many other special people and places who are also included in this memoir as beloved characters. I appreciate every resident and friend from our old neighborhood and from my school days, and every aunt and uncle and cousin. I appreciate the house I grew up in, Carlisle Avenue itself, Racine as I remember it, and the Wisconsin farms we visited. I love to remember it all.

.   .   .

And then, thank you to my dear, dear friends and relatives who listened to the early stories, wanted more, and have now waited for this book. You know who you are! You all have taught me so much about friendship.

And finally I turn with the greatest appreciation to my husband John, who I met one summer night in 1965 on a walk down Carlisle Avenue. (How fitting that we would meet on Carlisle Avenue!) From that night on, he has understood the love I have had for my parents. And I likewise turn to our wonderful daughter Lisa, who embraces our family history and responds with her powerful, loving challenge for me to write it.

Most of all, though, John and Lisa have given me our own home of love to cherish. From that gift comes the peace to look at the past and the courage to face the future.

Carol Burow Gianforte
February, 2015

~ Questions For Discussion ~

1. In this memoir, the author welcomes her memories. Describe the role of memories in your life.

2. The setting is central to the stories in this memoir. Describe the homes, streets or towns that are significant in your memories.

3. The author's stories take place in Wisconsin. Explain if you believe that they depict life mainly in the Midwest or if they contain broad themes that also describe life elsewhere.

4. What were some unique characteristics of the author's family? How do they compare to those of your family?

5. What aspects of growing up in the 1950's and 1960's hold appeal for you? Do you believe that those aspects can be repeated in some form today? If so, in what ways?

6. The author describes moments in her childhood that she vividly remembers today, such as the touch of her mother's hand. What are moments from your childhood that you vividly recall?

7. In the story "No Place Like Home," do you think that the camp nurse should have helped Carol return home? Why or why not? What would you recommend to a camp nurse today?

8. In the story, "Home for Christmas," do you think that Carol's parents should have allowed her to travel to New York City at her age? Why or why not? What would you recommend to parents today?

9. The story "Walking Through My World," emphasizes the freedom that children had to explore. Describe your favorite childhood explorations. What benefits were derived from this freedom?

10. The author's memoir emphasizes her continuing connection with people and places from her past. Is staying connected to the past important to you? If so, how do you maintain the connection?

Carol Burow Gianforte divides her time between Scottsdale, Arizona, and her hometown of Racine, Wisconsin. She and her husband have one daughter. *My Heart Leads Me Home* is Ms. Gianforte's first book.

CONTACT THE AUTHOR:
gianforteproductions@gmail.com

~ Praise
for
My Heart Leads Me Home ~

"Gianforte's delightful stories open the door to an incredible journey back in time to growing up in the 1950's and 1960's. You as the reader will stop every so often to look back at your own life's experiences with a smile. Every story will tug at your heart strings."
>   -Jean Davidson, author
>   *Growing Up Harley-Davidson* and
>   *Harley-Davidson Family Memories*

.   .   .

"Gianforte's memoir brings to life charming scenes of her parents and neighbors. You feel as if you know them all and have visited Carlisle Avenue yourself. Captured as well are the deep values and traditions of that 1950's Midwestern life."

~Kiki Swanson, author
Remnants, Ready for New Life, and
Tomorrow, Ready or Not

. . .

"Open this book and take an unforgettable trip down memory lane. You will only be disappointed when it ends."

~Terry Lynch, author
But I Don't Want Eldercare!

. . .

"Gianforte has absorbed so many physical presences and feelings from her youth, and then shaped them on paper so that the reader can enter those same rooms and share those experiences. There's a gentle warmth here that is very appealing."

~Mary Gardner, author
Milkweed, Keeping Warm, and
Boat People

. . .

"When I read Ms. Gianforte's stories, I feel as if she is telling them to me as we sit by a cozy fire. I step into the past as I hear her beautifully describe her feelings for her home, her family, and her neighborhood. It is an experience not to be missed!"

~Jessica MacPhail, Director
Racine Public Library

. . .

"Ms. Gianforte's memoir presents a poignant reminiscence of her Wisconsin girlhood home. The reader is taken on a magical journey back to the 1950's and 1960's to the people and places along her tree-lined boulevard. When her widowed father dies in 1995 and she locks the door at 1418 Carlisle Avenue for the last time, the reader wishes it were not so."

~D.W. Rozelle, author
The Kid who Climbed the Tarzan Tree

. . .